D1131002

Sing Us A Story

Sing Us A Story

Using Music in Preschool and Family Storytimes

by JANE MARINO

H.W. Wilson / 1994

Library of Congress Cataloging-in-Publication Data

Marino, Jane.
    Sing us a story : using music in preschool and family storytimes
/ by Jane Marino.
        p.   cm.
    Includes bibliographical references and index.
    ISBN 0-8242-0847-1
    1. Music—Instruction and study—Juvenile. 2. Education,
Preschool. 3. Children's songs. 4. Games with music.
5. Storytelling. I. Title.
MT1.M153   1994
372.87'044—dc20   93-6389
                                                            CIP
                                                            MN

Photographs by Lester Millman

To my husband,
Jim,
and my children,
Laura, Anne, and Paul

CONTENTS

Part V Resources

ACKNOWLEDGEMENTS

Thanks and salutations to the audiences, young and old, large and small, who have been part of my programs, sung with me, overlooked my mistakes, and applauded my successes. The joy I have felt in doing programs with them was my inspiration for writing this book. Thanks and love to Dorothy F. Houlihan, who can indeed carry a tune and much more, for being my partner in so many of these programs; and for her thoughtful reading of this manuscript and her valued suggestions. Thanks to my editor, Judy O'Malley, for her care, precision, and patience. Thanks to the administration and staff of the White Plains Public Library for their continued encouragement of and patience with my writing endeavors, especially the entire Children's Room Staff and Charlotte Szabo. Thanks to my family for their love and pride in me.

The author is grateful for permission to use:

"All God's Critters Got a Place in the Choir" words and music by Bill Staines. Copyright © 1978 by Mineral River Music BMI.

"Canoer's Lullaby" from *Travelling Home*, recorded by Cathy Winter. © 1987 Flying Fish Music.

"Down on Grandpa's Farm" traditional song, this version found in *The Second Raffi Songbook*, Crown, 1987. Song arrangements copyright © 1985 by Homeland Publishing, a division of Troubadour Records, Ltd.

"Garden Song" by David Mallett. Copyright © 1975 Cherry Lane Music Publishing Company, Inc. Used by permission.

"Skeleton Bones" from *The Holiday Song Book*. Copyright 1977 by Robert Quackenbush. Reprinted by permission of the author.

"So Long My Mom" by Bill Harley. BMI © copyright 1992 Round River Music.

"Time to Sing" music by Raffi/words by Raffi, D. Pike, and B. & B. Simpson. © 1985 Homeland Publishing, a division of Troubadour Records Ltd. All rights reserved. Used by permission.

"Whippily, Whoppily, Whoop" from *The Holiday Song Book*. Copyright © 1977 by Robert Quackenbush. Reprinted by permission of the author.

"You'll Sing a Song and I'll Sing a Song" words and music by Ella Jenkins. Used by permission of Ell-Bern Publishing Company, Chicago, Ill.

INTRODUCTION

Music, in all its forms, has the power to extend to every part of our lives. The emotions it elicits can range from the purest of joys to the most heart-wrenching of sadness. A mother soothes her infant with a lullaby. We sing "Happy Birthday" to friends and look forward to hearing it. Families sing their way through long car rides. Children sing their way through school from kindergarten to graduation.

From the simplest schoolyard chants to the most elaborate operatic arias, music has found its way into every medium. Tots who are not yet reading can sit down at computer games and know when they pick the right answers because music plays when they are right. Commercials have jingles to sell their products; television shows have opening themes to identify themselves. Music surrounds us in all its forms.

This book invites you to take just a part of the world of music and bring it past library doors, into nursery schools, and into classrooms. When you sing a song you are telling a story that is set to music. But the song has its own power to set in motion a series of links. Your song creates a link between you and the children you are singing with. The song also creates a link between them and the music. When you introduce children to songs, you are giving them a gift. You are giving them a way to share in it and become part of the music.

It doesn't matter if the song is new or an old favorite. And once it's a favorite, it remains so. The song also creates a link between stories or books. It can reinforce the message in a book or bridge two stories. Finally, it is a link between the program you do now and the next one. Music's power will work to extend the magic of this storytime past its end.

Librarians, teachers, and other people who work with children have a

unique opportunity to use music's power and bring its joy to the children they see every day. As more than just a repository of books, libraries have long taken the role of promoting programming of all kinds for both children and adults. They are, many times, centers for all kinds of entertainment and cultural events. By adding music to storytimes and other programs that are already in place for children, libraries can take an even more active role in introducing music to children.

Why sing? Why use music in a program at all? You can share stories successfully with children without singing a note. Many people do. But they are leaving out an element that will make their stories and books even more successful and memorable than they were. If you sing the song about "Five Little Monkeys Jumping on the Bed," there will be a spark of recognition when you read the picture book of the same name by Eileen Christelow (Clarion, 1989). If you sing a song about animals or farms, children will point out the animals they just sang about when you use a book like Margaret Wise Brown's *The Big Red Barn* (Harper & Row, 1989).

This book will examine the importance music can assume as a storytelling and programming tool and the role it can play any time children and grownups congregate to enjoy stories and rhymes. The first part of the book will take a look at preschool programming and suggest ways to introduce music into preschool programs, defined here as programs serving children from the approximate age of two-and-one-half to four. With a collection of songs suitable for preschoolers as well as picture books that have been successful for that age group, ideas on ways to combine those two winning elements will be suggested to make them even more successful.

This first group of songs contains thirty-eight that are appropriate for preschoolers. Although they are just a fraction of the vast array of songs available for this age range, all of these contain important elements that have made them successful. Their melody and lyrics make them easy to sing and remember, both for you and the children you are singing with. Their adaptability to many situations will give you the freedom to improvise. In many of the songs, the invitation to participate in some action, large or small—from waving and nodding to spinning and jumping, gives them an added whole-body dimension and physical reinforcement.

There may be other songs, perfect for preschoolers, that may have been equally successful for you and are not included here. Continue to sing them as you try the songs contained here and your list of favorites will keep growing. Don't forget to tap into the thousands of other songs that can be found in the many song collections for children that are available. There is a list of some reliable Song Collections in the back of this book. Singing with children is a process that always changes and grows.

The melody and lyrics of the songs included here work so well that many of the children that I have met in preschool programs sometimes only remember the songs or they remember them more than anything else.

One child whom I saw for several consecutive sessions had, I discovered one day, no idea of my name or the name of the program. But he knew that I was the lady who did "The Hokey Pokey"!

Another little girl came with her grandma, whom she was visiting, for our preschoolers' program. She sat quietly throughout the program while the rest of the group sang songs, seemingly with no response, much to her grandmother's initial dismay. But her grandmother later reported to me that "The Wheels on the Bus" was all she could talk about for weeks afterward. Fortunately, her grandmother had found it easy to learn and remember, and could sing it with her. Even after the little girl went back home to Boston, it continued to be the song several months later that she wanted everyone to sing with her again and again.

Some songs are more than songs. They are pretend games—a favorite activity for the preschool crowd. Their ability to pretend knows no limits. Many times, children come to one week's program sporting completely different names than they had used the week before. And some of them sound strangely familiar. Sam, for example, announced very seriously one week that he was "Tigger" today, and that his baby sister was "Eyeore." The next week he was something completely different. Sara will always turn to her Mom while she's in the library and say, "Let's pretend that we are . . . ," and usually she's worked out an entire scenario in her head, to which her mother good-naturedly agrees.

So it would be hard to find any group of preschoolers who would hesitate when invited to pretend to make the sun shine, plant a garden, go on a picnic, or ride on a bus. It's natural to them; it's what they do all the time. It's how they learn about and make some sense of the world around them.

Dancing is equally popular with the preschool crowd so there is also a group of dancing songs included with the preschoolers' songs. Simple to follow and fun to do, they will encourage a preschool group to try some moving around together.

The second part of this book will take a look at family storytimes and propose ideas for introducing and using music in programs where adults and children of all ages gather for stories and songs, whether it be in a library setting, at school or as part of organizations' functions. As versatile as they were for preschoolers, in this context songs can serve to introduce, to link, and to reinforce stories. Songs can themselves tell stories or they can draw the group together by inviting them to sing along with you.

Included here is a second group of songs which have been used successfully for our Family Storytimes. The mixture of such different ages in a Family Storytime group makes for a unique and amazing audience. With their parents along with them, younger children listen better to stories for which they might not otherwise have had the patience. Older children, who might squirm uncomfortably at first, thinking they've been roped into a "baby" program, feel increasingly more at ease when they see that there are all ages around them. And parents, some of whom have never been to such a storytime before, are an appreciative and eager audience.

Many of the thirty-nine songs included in this section are equally suited to school-aged groups, classes, or groups of adults. The longer songs spin yarns and tell sagas; the sing-along songs are both short and long, and their silly lyrics slip over the tongue and make us smile, and there are even some soothing lullabies included, as calming when used with family groups as they have been for generations in the nursery.

But although the songs are divided into two sections, that's not to say that the one section should never be mixed with the other. Quite the opposite. As flexible and adaptable as these songs are, many of them can be used in any number of situations. More than a few of them have already found their way into both sections of this book. But although it's true that they might have adapted slightly different dress in each section, they can change their attire to suit any occasion. The words suggested for each context are the words I chose to sing with them. Luckily for you, there's no rule that dictates how, or when, or where, any of these songs can be sung.

So, if you think you'd like to try "Frog Went A'Courtin" or substitute the more traditional lyrics of "Skip to My Lou" for preschoolers instead of the action verses suggested for them here, please do. And if you think that "Ducks Like Rain" will fit perfectly into your next storytime at which only older children or families will attend, that's terrific. Mix and match these songs any way you like.

Many of the songs included in both sections are folk songs, sung for many generations in many situations by regular folks who gave no thought to anything other than expressing their lives in song and enjoying the result. They were not concerned with their singing ability or lack of it.

What was important to them was enjoying—and sharing—the song. That was lucky for us because now they are still around for us all to enjoy. I hope sharing and enjoying these songs will become the idea that is most important to you as well. You may have an absolute lack of faith in your ability to sing. You may think, as a friend of mine says, that you can't carry a tune in a bushel basket! But the first time you try a song and children respond—and they will—you will change your tune.

The reason that so many of the songs selected for inclusion here are folk songs is that they are uniquely easy to sing. I hope you will recognize many of the tunes, but music and chords are provided to help you with those you don't know. If you can't read music, seek out tapes that have the songs on them. There are resource lists in the back of this book for tapes that contain many of the songs used here. But perhaps you will remember some of the tunes from your childhood and plunge bravely ahead.

In planning a program for any age or mix of ages, add as much or as little music to your program as you feel comfortable using. In doing a program for preschoolers, you may only want to begin with one or two songs along with picture books, finger games, and flannel board or puppet stories. For a family story hour, or a school-aged group, you may only try one song the first time; one that you think everyone knows so they'll sing along with you.

But however you incorporate songs and no matter how many songs you sing, I hope you will find, as I have, that it can be a rewarding, habit-forming way of linking stories and people together. After you add one song to a story time you will find that you have tapped into music's power and you'll want everyone else to sing along.

PART I

Beyond Mother Goose Time:
Preschoolers in the Library

Programming for Preschoolers and Their Caregivers

No matter what your experience may be in working with children, you will quickly discover when you do a program with a group of preschoolers, that they are indeed a unique and amazing bunch. Full of energy, independence and inquisitiveness, they want to touch, to hold, to climb over, to sit on, to try everything and anything. As they grow and discover the world around them, they are as mercurial as the weather: both sunny and stormy. They can be open and loving one minute and private and silent the next. They can be ready to share and be part of a group one day and be territorial the next.

In the library, they are eager to sing and listen to stories, but usually not without a grownup reassuringly close by. If you have had any experience with infant programming and have perhaps already met some of these children in that capacity, you will quickly discover what a difference a year or six months—or even less—can make. By the time they are around the age of two and-a-half to three, they are ready to climb off their parents' laps and assert their own personalities.

Although the parent or caregiver is just as important in this kind of program as they were in infant programming, their role has changed. Parents and caregivers are participating not *for* their children as they sometimes did in an infant program, but *with* their children. When they are encouraged to participate in the program with their child they show their two-and-a-half to four-year-old how to listen, how to sing along, how to participate. Although you and the caregivers want each child in the group to assert and enjoy his or her own personality and independence, grownups sometimes need to remind preschoolers that they are also part of a group. So, when a parent, grandparent, or a babysitter acts as a part of the group

and claps, sings, and dances along, chances are better that their pre-schooler will do the same.

Try to be as clear as possible when you explain to the caregivers in your group that you need and want their participation to make the experience a success for everybody. For many caregivers, this program may be their introduction to libraries and library programming. If this is their first child, they may have only just discovered that programs like yours exist and they are usually thrilled with this discovery. If they have older children, they may have only used the library as a source for homework help or as a reading resource. Keep those caregivers in mind as you begin your program planning. Their perceptions of libraries and library programs are usually far different from those of the people who have made your programs a regular habit. So be as clear and complete in your explanations as you can. Don't hesitate to include little details that you might think people would take for granted, even at the expense of asking your regular patrons to listen to information they've heard many times before.

As a programmer, you will often find yourself walking a fine line between maintaining a comfortable level of control over the group without letting that concern for control override all else. Many times, the planning that goes into your program will determine its overall success. It's important to lay the right groundwork so that everyone, both public and staff, understand the program's goals. Once it's clear to everyone why the program has been established, who it's intended for, and what happens during the program, once the program begins, all that's left is the enjoyment.

Happily, many libraries have some kind of preschool program already established. Of course, they come in many shapes and sizes, from weekly storytimes, to puppet and craft programs. If such is the case for you, your library is already working to address itself to the needs of that population, so you may not have to concern yourself with as many details of program planning as you would with a brand new program. But even when you are revamping an existing program, it's best to plan as thoroughly as possible.

Planning and Establishing
A Preschool Program

In planning any program for preschoolers, whether you are adding a new and different program to what is already in place or changing the aims and scope of an existing program, remember to determine clearly in your own mind the parameters of what you'd like to do so you can work within those guidelines. Some of these parameters can be defined by addressing yourself to the size of the group, its age range, the program's location, its frequency, and its nature.

In looking at every aspect of the program, try to consider the various issues you might face. In considering location, for example, you may have space limitations and you need to think about details like access for strollers, room for siblings (both younger and older), and friends. You need to establish age limits, both minimum and maximum. But at the same time, try to maintain a consistent, but not rigid, policy about those age limits. Try to remember that there will always be exceptions to every age rule.

In your zeal to plan as thoroughly as possible and prepare for any contingency, try not to set rules or put limits that are so hard to follow parents will feel they must lie in order to attend or that it's easier not to attend at all. The ongoing success of your program will depend in large part on the happiness of its participants. If they feel welcome and think you are happy to see them, they will keep returning to the program. And you *will* be happy to see them if the problems and details have all been worked out ahead of time. Let's examine a little more closely some of the questions that will help your planning.

Where Will This Program Take Place?

One of the keys to successful adult participation in your program will be the program's location and how you manage that location. If you are lucky enough to have a separate programming room or area, it will be easier for you to mark a clear beginning and end to the program. When you can separate your program from the rest of the library, the number in the group can be clearly defined and once they are settled, they can focus on and then participate in the program at hand. If this location is a room or area that is new to you, take a look at it, if you can, before you use it. If it's a small area, try to make sure that everything possible is removed so it is as clear and free of distractions as you can get it. If it is large, especially if it is too large for the group, try to define a small area of the room that is for your program, so the group's attention is drawn away from potential distractions and little ones are not tempted by far corners of the room to which they might wander.

If your program takes place in the library itself, you will have to deal with both the program's participants and other patrons who are using the library. The group's definition may become blurred and people will be more apt to join or leave the group during the program. These drifters can become a source of distraction for the rest of the group and lessen everyone else's participation. So consider how, and if, you can deal with both distractions as well as the higher level of extraneous noise that will inevitably occur in such an environment. It's easy for a good program to be adversely affected by unwanted and uncontrolled noise. One possible solution is to offer the program on a day or time that is normally not a busy one, so the only traffic in the library will be for the program. If the room is still busy, try to have another staff person on hand to remind the other patrons that a program is underway and their help and understanding would be appreciated. But if you find yourself coping with a noise factor no matter what, it helps if you make a general announcement, urging everyone's cooperation, before you start the program.

At What Age Group is This Program Being Aimed?

Although this may sound like a simplistic question for this toddler/preschool age range, it is an important point to be determined. Usually preschool programs are created for children who, generally defined, have outgrown infant programming, but who are too young for the longer, more structured storytimes aimed at the Pre/K–Kindergarten crowd. Age is a big consideration, both in your goals for and definition of the program and in the children's enjoyment of the program. So you will benefit in the long run from establishing a minimum as well as a maximum age for your group and sticking to it as closely as possible. The minimum age will have been selected based on your experience, or the experiences of others who preceded you in seeing how well a particular age range fared in the kind of program you are planning. Many programmers know only too well that children who are too young or even children who are "on the bubble," just turning two-and-a-half, do not have the socialization skills needed for this kind of preschool program. They will be unhappy during the program and both child and adult will leave with a bad experience.

Many babies who had loved the quiet, gentle atmosphere of an infant program, or who enjoy listening to stories and sharing songs one-on-one with a caregiver, can be initially intimidated by the large, active, lively group that awaits them at a preschool program. Many of them need to have a period of adjustment before they decide they like the program and can enjoy themselves. Those children who seemed so "old" in a Mother Goose Time program have now become the babies of this new group.

Parents may tell you that even though their child is not old enough, he or she is "ready" to move on. They may not understand that there is a minimum age and if they do, may even regard it as arbitrary and unnecessary. Assure them that their child will enjoy the program for their age, because it has been prepared for and is appropriate for their age. No matter how "ready" a child may appear, a little patience will prove to be in the parent's and child's best interest.

Sometimes, a child who is obviously too old for the program will surface. Usually, they are just older siblings, along for the ride and if you have the room, such older children usually enjoy themselves and will exert a positive influence on the group. But there are times when parents enjoy the program so much they keep bringing their child even when he or she has outgrown it. On an ongoing basis, this is usually not a good idea. An older child can dominate a group, shouting out answers or suggestions way ahead of the others. He or she, both in size and in ability may prove a divisive or distracting force for other smaller participants. A timely and gentle explanation to the well-meaning parent will usually bring an end to the problem, especially when there's an alternative, age-appropriate program.

For the child who is too old for a preschool storytime of the type discussed in this book, many libraries offer a more traditional kind of storytime. The program does not usually include a parent or other adult and in it, children, usually between the ages of four and six, listen to longer stories, combined with flannel boards, songs or finger games.

How Often Will the Program Be Offered?

Consideration of this point often leads to several other questions. Should you offer the program in a series that occurs once a week and lasts for four or six weeks with children registering for the entire series? This choice can allow you as a programmer a great deal of freedom within that given time frame. You can get to really know the children who attend and, as long as the group maintains a consistent and regular attendance, it will enable you to carry over songs, stories, and other ideas from week to week.

If you determine ahead of time the maximum number of children you can handle and establish that cut-off point, this kind of preregistration series means that, once registration is complete, you'll know exactly how many have signed up to attend all of the programs. This will eliminate a lot of headaches if limited programming space is a consideration. You can also accurately plan numbers of story mats, chairs, beanbags, name tags, instruments, or any other materials you need to use in the series.

Series programs have their disadvantages, as well. You must set up a workable registration policy and make sure any staff who may be involved are aware of it. There will also be a number of other questions to consider. How much time should you allow to take registration for such a program? How will registration be handled? Will there be any limitations on registrations and how will they be communicated to the public as well as staff? Even though many libraries have already determined the answers to these questions for other ongoing programs, it is probably a good idea for you to make sure about these points.

When registration is finished, you may find that children who are preregistered for a specific number of weeks may only show up for one or two weeks and then stop attending. So, even though you've planned for a specific size group, the number may in fact vary from week to week. Other than reminding parents as they register that the series runs for a set number of weeks, such variations in group size are hard to prevent. If you find yourself with the time and motivation to follow up with the no-shows and confirm that their interest has flagged, you might be able to allow other children to join the program. But if a change in size is not that big a problem for you, you may just want to work with whatever number attend.

If you are going to schedule additional series of programs throughout the year, there also needs to be a certain amount of down time between series, as well. Allow at least two weeks to plan and take registration for the next series. And although they might not seem like such a big disadvantage, it does take explaining to a public who eagerly looks forward to the next series to start.

If you choose not to run a series, what are the other alternatives? You may want to insert a regular ongoing preschool program into your programming schedule that requires no registration to attend. This may be the easiest course, if you have enough programming room and the number of children who attend is not a big consideration. A regular, ongoing program can be offered as often as time, staff, and energy considerations allow: once a week, once every other week, twice every other week. For a weekly or biweekly program, it could be offered once a day or, if possible, and if the number of participants warrants twice a day. If space is a worry and you don't have the staff or the patience to take registration, offering the program as often as you can should give your eager public the opportunities to take part in the program when they can.

In planning your schedule, try to find out what other kinds of programs are being offered in your community that might compete with yours, such as swimming, gymnastics or gymboree classes. Try to consider nursery school schedules as well. Some children in this age range attend two days a week, some three days. Listen to the parents who come into your library. They will be your best barometers of what days and times will be the most convenient and successful. Once the days and times of the program are clearly established and your public knows what they are, the attendance should fall into a fairly consistent pattern.

What Will Be the Content of Your Program?

Pages 36 to 83 offer the music and words for more than forty age-appropriate songs with suggestions for how to use them. They have been collected from many different sources. Ideas for using, interpreting and combining these songs are as varied as the people who sing them, so take some time to look through them carefully and note the different categories into which they have been grouped, as well as the order in which they appear here. It reflects the order in which they have proven to be the most successful during a typical program. Specifically, they are grouped into "Opening Songs," "Finger Games," "Imitation Songs," "Pretend Songs," and "Dance/Action Songs".

A brief definition and description of each category is given at the beginning of the Preschool Songs section on page 33. The philosophy for the selected order is simple. Like any other group of children, preschoolers need to warm up and warm to a program. So, if you plunge right in at the beginning of a program with a slam-bang dance or a long pretend song you won't get the same response as when you give everyone a chance to get settled and feel comfortable. Opening songs will help give them that chance. Their repetitious and sing-along nature allows preschoolers and their grown-ups to join in as little or as much as they want. It's a good idea to try two songs from this group in a program. So pair one song that you're fairly sure a lot of people will know like "Comin' Round the Mountain" with a song that might not be so familiar.

The Finger Games and Imitation Songs give you and your group a chance to get your fingers, your hands, and yourselves moving. These two groups of songs afford everyone a chance to join in with something they know and with which they are comfortable. "Two Little Blackbirds" with "The Wheels on the Bus" or "Lassie" will get everyone moving in some way. The process of singing as a whole-body experience is especially appealing for preschoolers but never loses its appeal for grown-ups, so it breaks the ice for everyone.

After everyone has moved around a bit, it's a good time to pretend a little. Go for a little ride, "Bumpin' Up and Down" in your wagon; dig in your garden; visit animals on a farm. Whatever you choose to try, involve the children as much as possible. They will connect to the activity and to you when you make them feel they are an important part of it.

Save the dancing or real action for last. "The Hokey Pokey" or "Jim Along Josie" acts as an effective finale and usually contains enough action to shake everyone loose. If you have enough room so your group can form a circle, that's usually the most fun. But try and dance even if you just don't have the room. Plan ahead of time how you will manage, but get everyone up and moving after you make sure there are no babies, books, or other assorted packages underfoot.

This is a starting menu for a primarily music-based program. The same format can also be used if you do not want to start out with quite so much music. You may want to leave out some of the songs suggested here and add more stories or finger plays instead. Two options are suggested here. One is a program that has only a little music, the other is entirely music-based. Although each contains suggestions for specific songs and/or stories to use, they need not be considered recipes to be followed to the letter. Rather, they are suggestions for ways to combine specific songs and stories that will give you a better idea of the kind of tasty programs you can cook up. Whether you copy them exactly or add a few ingredients of your own is not important. What is important is that you feel comfortable with the stories and songs you've chosen. If you do, they will work their magic for you and your group.

Song-Based Programs

Here are six songs that will work well together in a program.

"Time to Sing" and "She'll Be Comin' Round the Mountain" are effective opening songs for any program. The first is a Raffi song, and although it is not as well known as the second, a more traditional song, it is repetitive and easy to pick up. The lyrics "Time to sing . . . time to clap . . . time to say hello . . . " are tailor-made to get things moving. "She'll Be Comin' Round the Mountain" is a great sing-along to warm up everyone's voices and moods. You can use as many or as few verses or actions as you think everyone will enjoy. It's not a bad idea to start out slowly at first and build a repertoire of verses that everyone will join in singing.

"Two Little Blackbirds" is a finger game that can be sung, chanted or "told" as a small story. Repeat it a few times, with as many variations as you and your group can think up. Your birds can be blue or green, fast or slow, happy or sad. Don't worry about coming up with variations on what appears here, just ask for suggestions and your preschoolers will pick their own.

"Head, Shoulders, Knees and Toes" is a good way to move the group from just voices, fingers, and hands to a whole-body activity. Call it an exercise activity and do it twice. And while everyone is still standing up, sing "Mister Sun." It needs no other accompaniment than the actions

suggested. And if you still have the energy and want to dance, you can never go wrong with the "Hokey Pokey."

Even if you sing all six songs on this "menu," there will still be plenty of time to include stories in your program. This particular group of songs has no theme tying them together, so you have the freedom to choose whatever books you'd like. But, with another group of songs that might all be about animals, or colors, or counting, you could choose books appropriate to that idea. After the songs and stories, some kind of good-bye song or routine works well, even if it's only to "count" everybody who's attended, or to collect name-tags or whatever you've handed out. Your preschoolers will leave your program with melodies singing in their ears, ready to pick out some books to bring home with them.

Programs with Less Music Involvement

If you are not as comfortable using quite as many songs as the program outlined above suggests, sing a little less and put a little more emphasis on using picture books. There are plenty of wonderful picture books around which are suited to the two-and-a-half to four-year-old crowd.

A list of over fifty suggested picture books that can work well in preschool programs can be found on page 174. This list is annotated and each book has from one to three subject headings to help you in choosing them for your programs. A subject index for that purpose is located in the back of the book. The selection and use of these subject headings is very subjective and does not necessarily bear any resemblance to the Library of Congress or any other authority. They were chosen solely for the best ways those books could be used and combined in a storytime, both with each other and with songs. So you'll find *The Very Hungry Caterpillar* (Collins, 1979), for example, listed under the subject headings of food and numbers but it won't be under the heading of caterpillars. Look under gardens, trying, and families for *The Carrot Seed* (Harper, 1945), but you won't find it under carrots!

The list of books itself is also a subjective one, barely a sampling of the thousands of titles that are available. But these books have certain important and successful elements. They all contain bright, colorful illustrations that work well in group situations. Some books are larger in size than others, but even the smaller books, such as *Baby in the Box* (Holiday House, 1989) or *The Carrot Seed*, have illustrations that are large in proportion to their small size and can be seen easily from a distance. Their stories range from simple strings of phrases, like *Traffic, A Book of Opposites* (Crown, 1981), or *In My Garden* (Greenwillow, 1987), to more involved plot lines like *Ask Mr. Bear* (Macmillan, 1932), or *Caps for Sale* (W. R. Scott, 1947).

It's usually best to combine books that are on either end of both the length and plot scale, since preschoolers' attention spans are as mercurial as their natures. Just as they are learning to be a part of a group when they are singing and dancing, they are also still learning how to listen to a book in a group. Their enthusiasm will cause them to stand up and come over and touch the book, help you turn the pages, or comment on the plot. So you need to be as flexible as possible. Fortunately, books like *The Very Hungry Caterpillar* have pages you might want to invite preschoolers to touch and a story like *I Like Me* (Viking, Kestral, 1988), invites comments that are useful to the group. But other times, you need to exercise some gentle control and ask those enthusiastic preschoolers (or their grownups) to remember that it's time to listen.

If you want to combine more stories with just a few songs, try to bracket the stories with songs, rather than making your program a patchwork sampling. For example, if you start your program with an opening song like, "Time to Sing," follow it with a couple of books that have similar themes or plots and perhaps a finger play. Two books like *The Big Red Barn* (Harper & Row, 1989) and *Paddle, Said the Swan* (Atheneum, 1989), have the theme of farms and animals in common, and a story like "The Little

Red Hen," done with either a flannel board or with a book, can lead easily to songs like "When Ducks Get up in the Morning" or "Way Down on the Farm." Both lend themselves to plenty of imagination and participation after all the listening your preschoolers have done. And you can still introduce more action into your program with a dance like "The Hokey Pokey" and end your program with a song like "Skinnamarink."

Other Program Ideas

Many variations to the standard formula of songs and stories can add some spice to your preschool program. The four options offered here—flannel boards, puppets, bean bags, and instruments—are only a few of the ways many programmers and librarians are adding some variety to their programming. You may have some of these items available or perhaps your budget will allow you to buy some of them. Perhaps you can get a few donations, or you are handy enough to make some things like flannel figures or beanbags. By whatever means, if you are lucky enough to get any of these items, they will be worth the trouble for the many smiles they will bring to your group.

FLANNEL BOARDS. Preschoolers—and their parents—love to listen to stories told with flannel boards. They bring a different quality to stories than what is found within the pages of a book. You are able to move the characters around on the board, place characters together or in situations that may not occur in the book, and be a bit more flexible in the telling of the story.

The Flannel Board Storytelling Book by Judy Sierra (Wilson, 1987) contains easy-to-tell versions of several stories that are aimed at the preschooler age group, along with patterns, clear instructions on how to make flannel figures and helpful hints for telling the story. Stories like "The Three Billy Goats Gruff" or "The Little Red Hen" that lend themselves well to participation from the audience are always popular choices. If your budget is a bit more generous and you find yourself lacking in the basics to make flannel figures—time, patience, flannel squares, and a sharp pair of scissors—finished kits are available from some of the larger library and school media supply catalogs.

PUPPETS. Puppets have long been used in libraries on many levels, from full scale stage productions to the simple use of one puppet. Many librarians have the talent to take a simple puppet and, without benefit of stage, sound, lighting or props, transform a simple story into a three-dimensional experience. A simple caterpillar finger puppet weaving his way in and out of enlarged versions of the pages from *The Very Hungry Caterpillar* makes this story come alive for young listeners. A bear puppet, with the aid of a human friend, trying to put his clothes on all the wrong way like the bear in *How Do I Put it On* by Shigeo Watanabe (Philomel, 1979), is sure to produce peals of laughter and shouts of "No!" from delighted preschoolers who know very well that bear should put his cap on his head, not on his feet! But if your confidence in such talents is not intact, even holding a puppet or stuffed figure that resembles a character in the book you are reading can draw everyone's attention more sharply to the story. Many such character figures are available from catalog companies.

REALIA. Realia, here, is defined as those items that are usually considered as toys but when they are used within the context of programs, they become an integral part of them. Beanbags, for example, can be used quite effectively to become something more than beanbags. They become tools to explore different ways to move and follow direction. A song like "Put Your Finger in the Air" becomes "Put Your Beanbag in the Air." Beanbags do not fit as neatly on cheeks or chins the way fingers do, and the differences between them is in itself a discovery. But it's one that's fun to make.

Instruments are another kind of realia that add an extra dimension of discovery to your music program. When preschoolers are given the opportunity to "play" instruments together two simple but important things occur. Rhythm instruments become more than just noisemakers. They enable and allow preschoolers to become part of the program, mimicing the rhythm of the song as they join in. The instruments also give them the opportunity to function as a group. When instructed, they can and will begin and end at the same time. With a group that is comfortable with you, you can extend the use of instruments to include such concepts as soft and loud, or fast and slow. Or perhaps you don't want to "teach" them anything at all. Then, just let them play away. Instruments can become as important or as incidental as you want them to be.

As with flannel board kits, instruments of all kinds and all price ranges, are available from library and school media catalogs. Brightly colored tambourines shaped like bears, bells with monkey faces, rhythm sticks,

cymbals, castanets, blocks, and maracas that resemble frogs are among the many simple instruments available. They can be ordered individually or in many different-sized sets. An "Instrument Song" is included here on page 58, but almost any song can be used while playing instruments. How about, "If you're happy and you know it, play your instrument"?

If you plan to include any of these items in your program, remember to plan for logistics. Such "extras" will be an attractive addition to your program, but they will be even more attractive and tempting to little hands if they are not in sight and within reach when they shouldn't be. So, have some place to stow your props when you're not using them so they don't become a source of distraction. Keep that puppet out of sight until it's ready to tell its story. Turn the flannel board around so it's not facing the group and have the flannel figures laid out neatly, out of sight and in the order you'll need them for the story you're going to tell.

Try to find a cupboard or even a big box to keep instruments, bean-bags, flannel board and figures stashed, out of sight, until you are ready to include them in the program. It's awkward to stop and set up the flannel board and figures, so make sure they are ready at the beginning of the program. When the flannel board story is over, turn the board around again, so that, with its brightly colored figures, it is not a temptation. But anything that does not need prior attention, such as a puppet or instrument need not make an appearance until it is ready to be included in the program. So when that puppet has told his story, have him jump back into the box or bag or cabinet from where he came.

When including items that must be handed out, like beanbags or instruments, it's usually best for you, as the programmer, with maybe one adult volunteer helping, to hand them out to the preschoolers, rather than having the children come up to you. That will eliminate having little ones crowding around and the resulting chaos. When you are finished using the instruments or beanbags, you can collect them or, if it's the end of the program, invite the preschoolers to come up and put them in the desig-nated box themselves.

Music may already be an important part of your programs with your preschoolers or you may be slowly but surely adding music to a program that has had mostly stories. No matter where you are on that spectrum, this will be a process that will always change as long as you continue to do programs with children in this age group. Keep trying new stories and songs as well as different combinations of stories and songs so you can discover your own voice and be comfortable with what works for you.

It is always a good idea to have some kind of opening and closing routine that is similar enough from week to week to be familiar and recognizable to your group. It could be a favorite opening song that you always use. If you have name tags to hand out to the children, it could be as simple as a special hello to each child, saying their name. At the end, you may collect those name tags one by one, sing a good-bye song, or thank each child as they return bean bags or instruments. But as important as it is to keep your beginning and end fairly consistent, don't forget to keep adding some variety to the middle of your program. Using the same songs and stories constantly will make your presentation stale, and subsequently, will make the songs and stories seem stale. There are so many songs and stories available that it may seem overwhelming, so choose just one new thing to try every week. Make extra room in your schedule to practice that one new thing for each program so you'll always be assured of a touch of variety.

If you enjoy your preschoolers and the songs and stories you share with them, they will enjoy your program and they will return, eagerly looking for more. And the more you sing with them, the more you and they will enjoy getting together.

PART II

Preschool Songs

Different Ways to Sing with Your Preschoolers

Songs can invite preschoolers to participate, to pretend, to dance, to count—or just to sing. Songs can amuse, excite or calm. They can introduce stories or link them together. Or they can tell their own stories. But whatever the reason you choose the songs you want to share, your energy and enthusiasm will be the important elements that will make them a success.

To help you put songs together in a program, those included here have been grouped loosely into several categories. The first group is called "Opening Songs," but there are actually several kinds of songs included in this section. Some can be used to open your program, but others can be used to end it, and still others are just good sing-along songs. They all have classic melodies and easy-to-remember lyrics that make them songs you will want to repeat week after week and your preschoolers will come to recognize them and look forward to them each time.

The next group is called "Imitation Songs." They invite some kind of response from your preschoolers: clapping, reaching, tapping, etc. A small selection of "Finger Games" is also included. Although they are also found in *Mother Goose Time*, they become more interactive here and sometimes have slightly more involved directions to be used with this age group.

"Dance/Action Songs" are those that elicit more movement from your preschooler and will also call on them to act as part of a group as you all dance (or walk or hop) together. "Pretend Songs" invite young imaginations on a trip that can last as long or go as far as their young minds will allow, whether it's a trip on a red wagon, a ride on a bus, or a walk in the park.

All the songs have music in the form of a single line, right-hand melody with, for the most part, suggested guitar chords included as well.

Following the music for the first verse and chorus (if any), the words for additional verses will be given. For finger games, and other songs with actions, the words to verses will be repeated, along with any suggested actions. In the "Finger Games" section, there are no chords given, since the emphasis is on the actions and it's pretty difficult to play guitar while doing the actions suggested!

With or without accompaniment, and whatever you might call them, I think you will find these songs immensely adaptable. They can open your program, invite your preschoolers to imitate, to pretend, and to participate —all at the same time.

But whatever these songs invite you to do and wherever they take you and your preschoolers, the trip will be memorable: It always is when it's time to sing.

While six of the songs in this group work best at the beginning of a program, they can find a place any time you feel like singing them. They have lots of repetition, some action, and plenty of fun. Use them as openers, closers, or even in the middle. The last song in this section is a great choice to end your program.

Time to Sing

It won't take many sessions before your preschoolers will be singing, clapping, and tapping along with this song. But even the first time, it'll be easy for them to join in the "Hey, hey!"'s along with you.

Additional verse:

It's time for us to tap our toes
Together with our feet.
Time for toes to tap awhile.
Hey, Hey, Hey.

Toddler Time

Although this song is titled, "Toddler Time," you can easily change the name so it can suit your own program. "Story Time" or "Singing Time" or "Preschool Time" fit into the same music just as easily. It's a song that involves as much action as it does introduction.

Additional verses:

Clap your hands along with me.
Clap your hands, now, one, two, three.
It's as fun as it can be.
Clap hands—It's Toddler Time.

Reach your arms away up high.
Reach them up, try and touch the sky.
Reach as high as they will go.
Reach up—It's Toddler Time.

Stand up now, nice and tall.
Stand up with me, one and all.
Stand as tall as you know how.
Stand up—It's Toddler Time.

Let's do something quietly.
Tiptoe softly now with me.
Tiptoe softly as can be.
Tiptoe—it's Toddler Time.

Sit back down along with me.
Sit down cozy as can be.
Sit down ready to sing with me.
Sit down—It's Toddler Time.

Repeat first verse.

My Daddy and Me

Any grown-up could be inserted for "Daddy" in this song that could be used for opening—or closing—a program. You could sing about a preschooler's "Mommy" or "Grandma" or whoever. This is a great song to take you into a program, or to take a child out of the library and into the car, to sing on the way home—or on the way to the library on the next visit.

I'm in the Mood

With lots of repetition to make it a perfect sing-along, this is another good song to open a program. It also has lots of opportunity for as much moving as you want to include. With its invitation to sing, clap or sway, it's a sure bet to get all your preschoolers in the mood for fun.

I'm in the mood for clapping . . .

I'm in the mood for swaying . . .

Hey Dum Diddeley Dum

Although this song is also included in the Family Silly Songs section (page 148), with a bit more preparation, it is just as effective with pre-schoolers. If you rehearse the nonsense words in its chorus before you sing it with your preschool group, they will enjoy it much more. The chorus is just four words: "Hey, dum, diddeley," and "dum." Say each word separately and then the whole line together with the children before singing.

Don't worry about singing all the verses (though there are only three) that are included in the Family Silly Songs version; instead, do more repetitions of the chorus and, with a slight change, make one of the verses a bit more interactive, as suggested below.

She'll Be Comin' Round the Mountain

A standard sing-along that's always a hit, this can be a song about trains or wagons or just plain fun. At the end of each verse, add some kind of action or noise, such as the ones suggested here. If you are using this song with older children, or experienced singers, you can make this a cumulative song by repeating the sound for each of the verses already sung before adding the new sound for the latest verse. ("Toot, toot," "Whoa, back"; "Hi, there," etc.) This can get pretty complicated with preschoolers, however, so save on frustration and only try it if you think it will work.

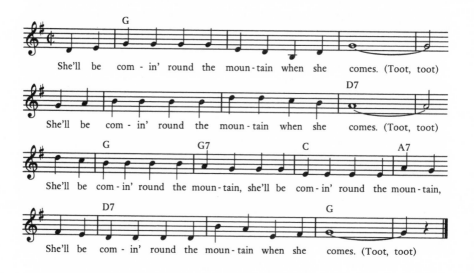

She'll be com - in' round the moun - tain when she comes. (Toot, toot)

She'll be com - in' round the moun - tain when she comes. (Toot, toot)

She'll be com - in' round the moun - tain, she'll be com - in' round the moun - tain,

She'll be com - in' round the moun - tain when she comes. (Toot, toot)

She'll be drivin' six white horses when she comes
    (Whoa, back!)
She'll be drivin' six white horses when she comes
    (Whoa, back!)
She'll be drivin' six white horses, she'll be drivin' six white horses,
She'll be drivin' six white horses when she comes. (Whoa, back!)

And we'll all go out to meet her when she comes
    (Hi, there!)
Yes, we'll all go out to meet her when she comes
    (Hi, there!)

Yes, we'll all go out to meet her, yes, we'll all go out to meet her,
Yes, we'll all go out to meet her when she comes,
    (Hi, there!)

Additional verses:

She'll be wearing old red flannels when she comes, (Scratch!,
    scratch!) . . .

Oh, we'll all have chicken and dumplings when she comes (Yum!
    Yum!) . . .

We'll be singin' Hallelujah when she comes (Hallelujah!)

The Wheels on the Bus

As you can see, many of these verses lend themselves to wonderfully creative play-acting as you and your group can pull back on your reins, wave a big "Hi," scratch your sides and rub your full "tummies."

Of course, no preschool program would be complete without the hands-down favorite imitation sing-along, "The Wheels on The Bus." I've only included the top ten favorite verses.

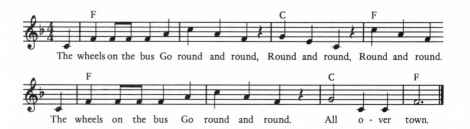

The wheels on the bus Go round and round, Round and round, Round and round.
The wheels on the bus Go round and round. All o - ver town.

Additional verses:

The wipers on the bus
Go swish, swish, swish. .

The doors on the bus
Go open and shut. . .

The money on the bus
Goes clink, clink, clink. . .

The horn on the bus
Goes beep, beep, beep. . .

The driver on the bus
Says move on back. . .

The kids on the bus
Go yakkety, yak, yak. . .

The babies on the bus
Go wah, wah, wah. . .

The grownups on the bus
Go shh, shhh, shhhh. . .

The people on the bus
Go up and down. . .

Finger Games

Since by definition, "finger games" involve using your fingers or your hands, they naturally lead to many games involving "five," whether they are five kittens or ducks or peas or pumpkins. Sometimes, there are "two," since there are two hands. And sometimes, finger games use the number "six," as one does here. Finger games often seem to involve animals, as you can see in the first three included here; other times, they are about family members. Or maybe they are just about fingers!

Two Little Blackbirds

This first song can evolve from a simple finger game to a saga for preschoolers. After a few turns at this song, or rhyme if you prefer to chant it, as soon as you make two fists with your hands, they will shout out, "birds!" and pop their knees up to make hills for their birds to perch. Possibilities abound. The birds can be blue or black or any color at all. They can be fast or slow, high or low, sleepy or speedy as they "fly away" and then "come back." In fact the only trouble you may encounter is how to end this so you can move on to something else.

Two lit-tle black-birds Sit-ting on a hill, One named Jack, The oth-er named Jill.

Fly a - way, Jack. Fly a - way, Jill. Come back, Jack. Come back, Jill.

Two little blackbirds	Make fists with hands with thumbs up.
Sitting on a hill,	Put fists on knees.
One named Jack,	Lift one fist.
The other named Jill.	Lift the other fist.
Fly away, Jack.	One bird behind back.
Fly away, Jill.	Other bird behind back.
Come back, Jack.	Bring one bird front.
Come back, Jill.	Bring other bird front.

Five Little Monkeys

This rhyme works just as well, and is, in fact, better known, as a finger play. It's also been done, slightly expanded, as a picture book by Eileen Christelow that's great fun to read to a group who knows the finger play well (see Resources section, p. 176).

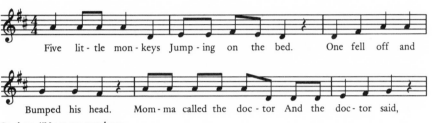

Five lit - tle mon - keys Jump - ing on the bed. One fell off and

Bumped his head. Mom - ma called the doc - tor And the doc - tor said,

Spoken: "No more monkeys
Jumping on the bed!"

Five little monkeys	One hand holds up five fingers.
Jumping on the bed.	The other hand is out flat, palm up.
	Two fingers jump on palm
One fell off and	And fall off.
bumped his head.	Tap head with hand.
Momma called the doctor	Pretend to phone.
And the doctor said,	Point finger and wag pointer
"No more monkeys	finger at children.
Jumping on the bed."	

Each verse is sung with one less monkey until there are no more monkeys left on the bed. Show the children how to make a "zero with their hands, by forming your hands into a big O and sing the final verse with them.

Now there's no more monkeys jumping on the bed.	Form a circle with fingers like the number zero.

Six Little Ducks

This will always be a hit with preschoolers. You'll turn them all into a bunch of "quackers"!

1. Six little ducks
    That I once knew:
    Fat ones, skinny ones,
    Fair ones too,

Chorus

But the one little duck
with the feather
On his back,
He led the others with his
quack, quack, quack!
Quack, quack, quack!
Quack, quack, quack!
He led the others with his
quack, quack, quack!

2. Down to the river
    They would go.
    Wibble wobble,
    Wibble wobble,
    to and fro.

Hold up six fingers
Point to self.
    Hold hands far apart,
    Then put them close together.

Hold up one finger
Wag hand behind back.

Open and close hand with a
    quacking motion on each
    "quack."

Chorus

3. Home from the river
    They would come.
    Wibble wobble
    Wibble wobble
    Ho, ho, hum.

Chorus

4. Repeat first verse and chorus

Come a Look a See

This finger game uses all five fingers, as each family member is identified, as well as both hands as the hands and fingers fold together in a "hug" on the last line. It usually requires more dexterity than little ones can muster. But don't let that stop you from using it. It's short and memorable enough that they and their grown-ups can bring it home. Nobody seems to mind if they can't get it just right at first and they have quite a good time trying.

Come-a-look-a-see, Here's my mom. Come-a-look-a-see, Here's my pop.

Come-a-look-a-see, Broth-er tall. Sis-ter, ba-by, I love them all.

Come a look a see,	Hold hands up, palms facing each other.
Here's my mom.	Touch thumbs together.
Come a look a see,	
Here's my pop.	Touch pointers together.
Come a look a see,	
Brother tall.	Touch middle fingers together.
Sister, baby,	Touch ring fingers, then pinkies.
I love them all.	Fold hands together.

Five Kittens in the Bed

One more finger game that involves five—kittens that is.

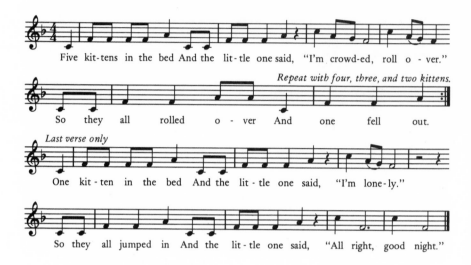

Five kit-tens in the bed And the lit-tle one said, "I'm crowd-ed, roll o - ver."

Repeat with four, three, and two kittens.

So   they   all   rolled   o - ver   And   one   fell   out.

Last verse only

One kit - ten in the bed And the lit - tle one said,   "I'm lone - ly."

So they all jumped in And the lit - tle one said,   "All right, good night."

Five kittens in the bed	Hold up five fingers,
And the little one said,	
I'm crowded, roll over	hunch shoulder together as if crowded.
So they all rolled over	Roll hands.
And one fell out.	Hold up one finger.
Four kittens in the bed	Hold up four fingers, repeat
And the little one said. . .	words and action as above.
Three kittens in the bed	Hold up three fingers. . .
And the little one said. . .	
Two kittens in the bed	Hold up two fingers. . .
And the little one said. . .	
One kitten in the bed	Hold up one finger
And the little one said	
I'm lonely.	Spread hands out, palms up.
So they all jumped in	Make arching motion with
And the little one said,	hand.

"All right, good night."   Nod head, then put hands to
                                  side of head and bend head
                                  to mimic sleep.

Fee, Fi, Fo, Fum

A short finger game about—fingers! Do it over and over. Your preschoolers will love it.

Fee, fi, fo, fum	Clap hands four times.
See my fingers	Wiggle fingers.
See my thumbs.	Wiggle thumbs.
Fee, fi, fo, fum.	Clap hands four times.
Goodbye, fingers.	Put one hand behind back
Goodbye, thumbs.	Put other hand behind back.

Five Little Pumpkins

This is also on page 152 as a Hallowe'en song. But toddlers love it anytime.

Five lit - tle pump - kins sit - ting on a gate. The first one said, "Oh my, it's get - ting late." The sec-ond one said, "There are witch - es in the air." The third one said, "But I don't care." The fourth one said, "Let's run and run and run." The fifth one said, "I'm read - y for some fun." Oo - oo, went the wind and out went the light. And the five lit - tle pump - kins rolled out of sight.

Five Little pumpkins	Hold up five fingers.
Sitting on a gate.	
The first one said,	Hold up one finger.
"Oh my, it's getting late."	Look at wrist.
The second one said,	Hold up two fingers.
"There are witches in the air."	"Ride a broom."
The third one said,	Hold up three fingers.
"But I don't care."	Shake head.
The fourth one said,	Hold up four fingers.
"Let's run and run and run."	Running motion with arms.
The fifth one said,	Hold up five fingers.
"I'm ready for some fun."	Point to self.
Oooh went the wind and	Spread hands out
Out went the light	Clap hands.
And the five little pumpkins	Hold up five fingers.
rolled out of sight.	Roll hands

Once your preschoolers are warmed up, it's time for a little imitation. As you can explain to your group, it's easy. All they have to do is what the songs tell them to do.

Clap Your Hands

Although only one verse is suggested here, many verses can be improvised. Stamp your feet, tap your toes, etc. You can expand the action of this song and get your group to walk around in a circle during the "la, la" section, or you can continue whatever action you've begun in the lyrics.

Clap, clap, clap your hands. Clap your hands to - geth - er. Clap, clap, clap your hands. Clap your hands to - geth - er. La la la la la la la La la la la la la la La la la la la la la La la la la la la.

Head, Shoulders, Knees and Toes

This song involves every part of you and becomes an exercise for the whole body.

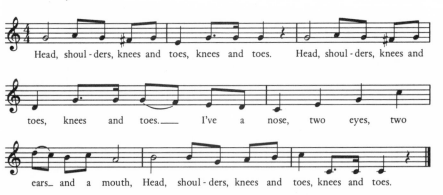

If You're Happy and You Know it

A classic, popular song that can fit almost anywhere in your program. Thanks to nursery schools, lots of kids already know it and even if they don't, its format encourages participation. Use it to open your program (If you're happy and you know it, say "Hello"), to close it (change the "Hello" to "Goodbye"), or anywhere in between.

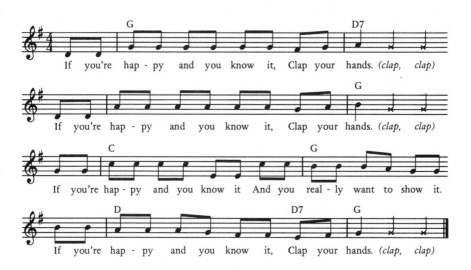

Additional verses:

If you're happy and you know it,
Shout hooray (*hooray!*). . .

If you're happy and you know it,
Blow a kiss. . .

If you're happy and you know it,
Give yourself a hug. . .

Put Your Finger In The Air

A standard that's fun for preschoolers, this is interactive without being too demanding and the humor is right on target.

Additional verses:

>Put your finger on your head,
>On your head. . .
>Tell me is it green or red. . .
>
>Put finger on your nose. . .
>Is that where the cold wind blows. . .
>
>Put your finger on your cheek. . .
>Leave it there about a week. . .
>
>Put your finger on your chin. . .
>Leave it out and never in. . .
>
>Put your finger on your shoulder. . .
>Oh it makes you look much older. . .
>
>Put your finger on your belly. . .
>Make it shake like apple jelly. . .

We Are All Clapping

In this song, the lyric reads ". . . at the library", but that can be easily changed depending on where you and your group actually are, whether it's ". . . at our house today" as the original version goes, or ". . . during storytime" or ". . . in our circle game" or ". . . in our group today" or ". . . at our school today."

Additional verses:

We are all stamping,
Stamp, stamp, stamping. . .
When you stamp with me . . . ,

We are all walking,
Walk, walk, walking. . .
When you walk with me . . . ,

We are all hopping
Hop, hop, hopping. . .
When you hop with me . . . ,

Lassie

Everyone will recognize the tune of this next song as soon as you start to sing. The words "this way and that way" cry out for actions large and small although bending to the front, then to the sides works well at the start. It's also fun to sing about "laddies" as well as "lassies." The variation, Instrument Song, is a perfect example of how well this timeless tune adapts to an endless number of situations. You can take that same tune and tailor it however you want. It will always fit perfectly.

Did you ev - er see a las - sie, a las - sie, a las - sie,

Did you ev - er see a las - sie, Go this way and that?

Go this way and that way and this way and that way.

Did you ev - er see a las - sie, Go this way and that?

Instrument Song

It's time to play your instruments,
Instruments, instruments,
Time to play your instruments,
Play them with me.
Play your tamborines,
Rhythm sticks,
Cymbals, and monkey bells.
Time to play your instruments,
Play them with me.

It's fun to play your instruments,
Instruments, instruments,
Fun to play your instruments,
As you can see.
Play your triangles,
Rhythm sticks,
Tamborines, maracas.
It's fun to play your instruments.
Play them with me.

It is, of course, easy to get carried away with this idea. . .

Stand up and play your instruments
Instruments, instruments.
Stand up and play your instruments,
Stand up with me.
Play your tamborines, triangles,
Rhythm sticks, monkey bells,
Stand up and play your instruments.
Stand up with me.

And it could go on and on until the end of your program. . .

It's time to say goodbye,
Goodbye, goodbye.
It's time to say goodbye,
Til we see you next time.

Mister Sun

The funny thing about making up different words for this song is that I always have grown-ups and children sing right along with me, even if they've never heard it before. That's how singable this tune makes any lyrics.

One day, a mother was seen entertaining her toddler with this song while waiting for their food in the middle of a shopping-mall eatery. A song with movements easy for even the youngest toddler to do, it is so portable you can use it to make the sun shine anywhere.

When using this song in a program, get your group to stand up and form a circle, if possible, to make the sun shine all around.

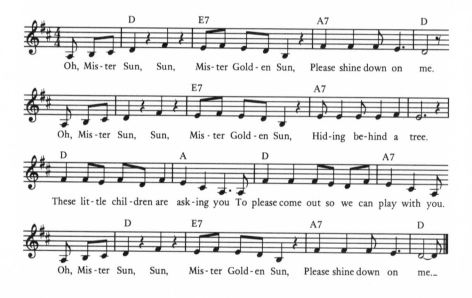

Oh, Mister Sun, Sun,	Hands above to form a circle.
Mister Golden Sun,	Lower arms
Please shine down on me.	Point to self.
Oh Mister Sun, Sun	Hold arms above head in circle.
Mister Golden Sun,	
Hiding behind a tree.	Put hands in front of face

These little children

Are asking you

To please come out

So we can play with you.

Oh, Mister Sun Sun,

Mister Golden Sun,

Please shine down on me.

Point to others in group beckon

    with arm

Point to group again.

Hold arms above head in circle.

Lower arms and point to self

Sharing songs with toddlers and preschoolers is a joy and presents an opportunity for lots of participation. Many of the songs included in this section need the children's participation to work, as you ask them to come up with animals to bring home, food to put in the picnic basket or animals they might see in the zoo. You may receive some surprising suggestions and the children get a chance to exercise their imaginations. Count on some creative pets!

The Baby Bumble Bee

This first song invites young listeners to use their imaginations and improvise. Instead of singing about a bumble bee, as the traditional version of this song does, you can expand the idea to sing about all kinds of animals. Suppose you found a baby rabbit, or a baby dinosaur, or a baby lion on the way home. Talk about how you would carry them home and how proud your Mommy would be.

Ask for or suggest ideas for animals and demonstrate to the children the idea of pretending to hold whatever baby animal they're bringing home. There are endless great possibilities in each idea and in each animal. And don't forget the sound each animal makes in the last line of each verse. The children will be happy to join in on the sounds each animal makes.

Additional verses:

I'm bringing home a baby dinosaur
Won't my Mommy be so proud of me
'Cause I'm bringing home a baby dinosaur.
Roar, roar, roar says that dinosaur.

I'm bringing home a baby tiger cub.
Won't my Mommy be so proud of me!
'Cause I'm bringing home a baby tiger cub.
Grr, grr, grr says that cub.

I'm bringing home a baby kitty cat.
Won't my Mommy be so proud of me!
'Cause I'm bringing home a baby kitty cat.
Mew, mew, mew says that cat.

Going To the Zoo

Tom Paxton is a master at making songs that kids love to join in and sing. This is one of them, and as with many good songs, there are any number of ways to sing it. You can sing the song the way it's shown here, with Paxton's wonderful words, or you can ask the kids to suggest some animals to sing about.

No matter how you sing this song, be sure to introduce it by telling the kids that they are about to take a pretend trip to the zoo. This will start them thinking about the kinds of animals that live there. So, if you do decide to ask them for suggestions, somebody will be ready with an idea.

Once they chime in, however, you need to switch on your imagination to complete the verse, usually by supplying a sound or action that the animal makes. For example, if someone says lions, ask the children to tell you what sound they make. That can lead to a verse like, "See all the lions roaring out loud." Or how about elephants "swinging their trunks"? Whatever animals you sing about, you'll have a great trip!

Additional verses:

> Look at all the monkeys swinging in the trees,
> Swinging in the trees, swinging in the trees.
> Look at all the monkeys swinging in the trees.
> We can stay all day.

Chorus

> Look we're going to zoo, zoo, zoo.
> How about you, you, you.
> You can come too, too, too.
> We're going to the zoo, zoo, zoo.
>
> Look at all the crocodiles swimming in the water,
> Swimming in the water, swimming in the water.
> Look at all the crocodiles swimming in the water,
> We can stay all day.

Chorus

> Repeat first verse.

Chorus 2X

Bumping Up and Down

This is a pretend song that will get the children moving and bumping. Before the song begins, practice "bumping," which is really bounding, with the children. Some of the preschoolers will be sitting in laps and the more independent children will be sitting on the floor on their own. Many times, lap sitters will be helped by their grownups to "bump," so it becomes shared fun. Even though they may start out slowly at first, with really lively groups, "bumping" sometimes turns into "jumping!"

Additional verses:

> One wheel's off and the axle's broken.
> One wheel's off and the axle's broken.
> One wheel's off and the axle's broken.
> Won't you be my darling?

> Let's all fix it with our hammer.
> Let's all fix it with our hammer.
> Let's all fix it with our hammer.
> Won't you be my darling?

> Bumping up and down in my little red wagon.
> Bumping up and down in my little red wagon.
> Bumping up and down in my little red wagon.
> Won't you be my darling?

In My Garden

What's more fun for a preschooler than digging in dirt? Actions to mimic digging, planting, hoeing, or eating make this a busy pretend song. This is arranged as originally written by Alan Arkin, with the melody line and key rising with every two verses, adding a note of energy as the pitch becomes higher and higher.

Verse 2. Hoeing, hoeing,
This is how we hoe the weeds. . .

Verse 4. Growing, growing,
This is how the peas will grow. . .

Verse 6. Eating, eating,
This how we'll eat the peas
From our garden. . .

Over in the Meadow

Another classic children's song, the words to the following can be found in many variations in countless collections, and in several picture book interpretations. Some of these versions are listed in the "Resources" section of this book. The words can be changed according to your taste in animals. You can have one duck quacking in the sand, in the sun, or four froggies hopping on the rocks by the shore. There are as many possibilities as there are animals.

And there are just as many ways to share this song. It's a song about animals, a counting song, or a song about the noises animals make, or the places animals live. It's even a song about moms and babies. It's fun to ask, after each verse's first line has been sung, "What sound does a frog or a duck or a bee make?" and the children become willing croakers, quackers or buzzers.

It could even incorporate colors if you use a flannel board to tell the story, adding the appropriate figure to the board with each verse.

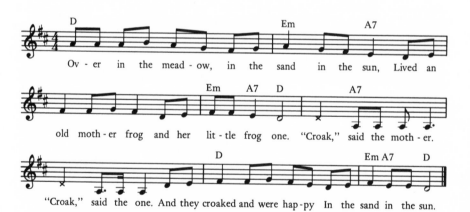

Additional verses:

> Over in the meadow, in the stream so blue,
> Lived an old mother fish and her fishes two.
> "Swim," said the mother. "We swim," said the two.
> And they swam and were happy
> In the stream so blue.

Over in the meadow, in a nest in a tree,
Lived an old mother bird and her birdies three.
"Sing," said the mother. "We sing," said the three.
And they sang and were happy
In their nest in the tree.

Over in the meadow, in a rock by the shore,
Lived an old mother snake and her wee snakes four.
"Hiss," said the mother. "We hiss," said the four.
And they hissed and were happy
In their rock by the shore.

Over in the meadow, in a big bee hive,
Lived an old mother bee and her little bees five.
"Buzz," said the mother. "We buzz," said the five.
And they buzzed and were happy
In their big bee hive.

Way Down on The Farm

A traditional song originally entitled, "Down On Grandpa's Farm," the title used here makes this imaginary farm belong to anyone and the animals that live there are limited only by your group's imagination! Like many good, classic children's songs, this one provides more than one avenue for vivid imaginations. As you and your group select the animals you want to sing about, this song can become a color game with brown cows, red hens, pink pigs and yellow ducks as well as a sound game with lots of mooing, clucking, oinking, and quacking!

Additional verses:

> Way down on the farm
> There is a little red hen. . .

Chorus

> Way down on the farm
> There is a little pink pig. . .

When Ducks Get Up in the Morning

Here is another animal song that is filled with opportunities for noisemaking and fun. Make sure your group understands that the animals' way of saying good day is by quacking, mooing, or whatever. Let them chime in with the appropriate sound after you say that those animals "always say, 'Good day'."

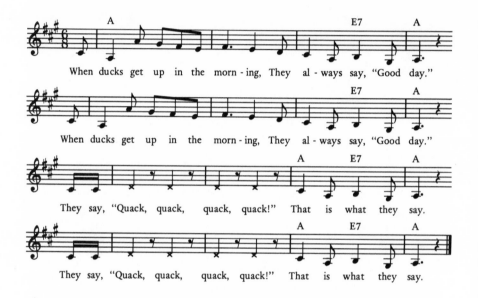

For additional verses substitute as many farm animals as you and your group have the energy for. It's fun to end with this verse:

When you get up in the morning,
You always say "Good Day."
When you get up in the morning,
You always say "Good Day."
You say
(*spoken*) "Hi, Mom!" "What's for breakfast?"
That is what you say. You say,
(*spoken*) "How are you?" "Good morning!"
That is what you say.

Many of the dance/action songs in these next few pages began as circle games or dances that had a great deal of courtship ritual attached to them, like "Go In and Out the Window," or were popular as playground games, like "Sodeo," or "There's a Brown Girl in the Ring." Using these songs in your preschool program brings their culture and history alive in your library and gives your preschoolers the opportunity to extend their imaginations and abilities to pretend.

Go In and Out the Window

This first song can trace its roots to various cultures, from Trinidad to Britain. But in every culture, though sometimes done as a courtship dance, sometimes a playground game, it has always been a circle game. To do this "dance" children would form a circle with one child weaving his way in and out of the children's raised, linked arms. But that method might not prove practical—or successful—in this kind of preschool program.

Instead, have the children and their grown-ups form a circle and lead them in a quiet dance that is very similar to an imitation song. On the words, "Go in and out the window," have everybody bend forward on "in" and then stand straight up on "out." You can improvise as many verses as you like, until you see which ones work and which do not. Go back to the chorus after each verse, if you like. Some suggestions for verses are included.

Additional verses:

Let's clap our hands together.
Let's clap our hands together.
Let's clap our hands together.
As we have done before.

Let's reach up to the ceiling. . .

Let's walk around the circle. . .

Now go back to your places. . .

There's a Brown Girl In the Ring

A song from the West Indies traditionally done with one child in the middle, the others forming a circle around her, it can be just as successful with you in the center suggesting different ways for your preschoolers to move. With its lively rhythm and tra-la-la's, preschoolers will be ready to show you their motions!

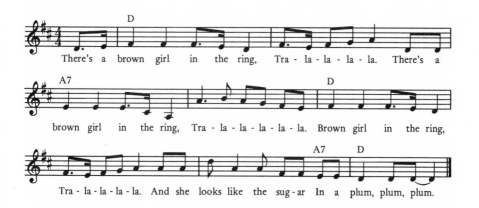

There's a brown girl in the ring, Tra - la - la - la - la. There's a brown girl in the ring, Tra - la - la - la - la - la. Brown girl in the ring, Tra - la - la - la - la. And she looks like the sug-ar In a plum, plum, plum.

Additional verses:

Now show me your motion,
Tra-la-la-la-la.
Now show me your motion,
Tra-la-la-la-la-la.
Show me your motion,
Tra-la-la-la-la.
And she looks like the sugar
In a plum, plum, plum.

Let's skip across the ocean,
Tra-la-la-la-la.
Let's skip across the ocean,
Tra-la-la-la-la-la.
Skip across the ocean,
Tral-la-la-la-la.
And she looks like the sugar
In a plum, plum, plum.

The Hokey Pokey

Once a slow, courtly dance and then a romp, this song had many names during its history, including "Hinkumbooby." But today, of course, any child can tell you its name is "The Hokey Pokey." Always a favorite, this dance will get everyone involved, even younger siblings who aren't quite sure what to "put in" and what to "shake all about"! As with so many other songs, you can extend (with your elbow, ear, shoulder) this dance as far as you want it to go.

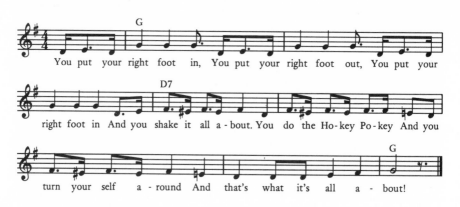

You do the Hokey Pokey
And you turn yourself around
And that's what it's all about.

Additional verses:

You put your left foot in. . .

You put your right arm in. . .

You put your left arm in. . .

You put your head in. . .

You put your whole self in. . .

Jim Along, Josie

Based—very loosely—on an old minstrel song, this piece of American folk music is constantly changing in tune and words. Many children's collections list a number of variations, including versions in which "Josie" is the dance itself—"Hold My Mule While I Dance Josie." There are any number of versions of "Hey, jim along," like "Hi, come along," or "Come-a-get along." So, feel free to improvise as you get your group moving, swaying, jumping or doing whatever it takes to have fun with the music.

Hey, jim a - long,   Jim a - long, Jo - sie, Hey, jim a - long,   Jim a - long, Joe.

Chorus (2x)
> Clap jim along,
> Jim along, Josie,
> Clap jim along,
> Jim along Joe.

Other ideas:
> Hop jim along
> Jim along Josie. . .
>
> Walk in a circle
> Jim along Josie. .

Chorus (2x)
> Jump, jim along,
> Jim along, Josie,
> Jump jim along
> Jim along, Joe.

A good ending verse:
> Back to your places,
> Jim along, Josie
> Back to your places,
> Jim along, Joe.
> Back to your places,
> Jim along, Josie,
> Back to your places,
> Cause it's story (sitting) time
> It's story (sitting) time.

New River Train

Here is another versatile folk song. The traditional lyrics in the first three verses will fall gently on preschoolers' ears, but the melody also allows for inventive fun. Instead of numbers, any name can be inserted, provided, of course, you have a rhyme to go with it. It also might be fun to walk around in a circle during the chorus, as your group becomes so many cars in a "train." Then, the last three verses can give you some action.

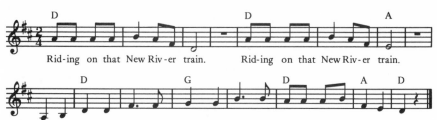

Rid-ing on that New Riv-er train.   Riding on that New Riv-er train.

It's the same old train That brought me here, And gon-na take me back a-gain.

Darlin', you can't love one
Darlin', you can't love one.
You can't love one 'cause it isn't any fun.

Chorus

Darlin', you can't love two.
Darlin', you can't love two.
You can't love two and still be true.

Chorus

Honey, you can't love three.
Honey, you can't love three.
You can't love three and still have me.

Chorus

Additional Verses

Clap your hands with me.
Clap your hands and you will see.
Just how much fun it can be.

Chorus

> Reach your arms way up high. . .
> Reach your arms way up high
> But don't say goodbye. . .

Chorus

> Jump up as high as you'll go. . .
> Jump as high as you'll go
> Just don't say no.

Shake My Sillies Out

A fun song for movin' and shakin', this song written and made popular by Raffi, can go on for as long as your listeners have the energy! You can make up as many verses as you like, adding bending, stretching, stamping, or whatever comes to mind.

Additional verses

> Gotta clap, clap, clap my crazies out. . .
>
> Gotta jump, jump, jump my jiggles out. . .
>
> Gotta yawn, yawn, yawn my sleepies out. . .
>
> Gotta shake, shake, shake my sillies out. . .

Skip To My Lou

Although the more time-honored and recognizable lyrics to this song (on page 113) work well both in preschool and in family singalong programs, the rhythmic tempo of the music and the easy-to-sing chorus also make this a circle dance with endless possibilities for adaptation.

Chorus

> Start your walking, Skip to my Lou,
> In a circle, Skip to my Lou,
> Keep on walking, Skip to my Lou,
> Skip to my Lou, my darling.

Chorus

> Stretch your arms and reach up high,
> Maybe we can touch the sky,
> You never know until you try,
> Skip to my Lou, my darling.

Down In the Valley

This has been a song-game played by African-American children for more than one hundred years. It has many different versions and today continues to be enjoyed by all children. Bring this song into your preschool programs and show everyone how good it can feel to "rise, Sally, rise." The words call for movement and improvisation. "Chug down" by pumping your arms back and forth and bending your knees as you sing the first verse. Then, chug back up on the second verse.

Sodeo

"Sodeo" is another song that does double duty, working well in Family Song and Storytimes and Preschooler programs. Here, used as a preschoolers' song, the words, "to the front, to the back, to the seesaw side" as well as the active verses will get your listeners to move. When it's time to walk during the song, you might want to point your preschoolers in one direction or the other to avoid confusion, and call out that it's time to stop and sing before each chorus, for the sake of order. But even with a minimum of direction, the song will work on its own and is sure to produce lots of fun.

Additional verses:

Turn around and walk the other way
It's time for us to walk the other way.
Follow around in the circle with me.
Follow around, now, one, two, three.

Chorus

Stand right there and
Keep your feet on the ground.
Now make a little circle by
Turning around.
Make a little circle,
Around you go.
That's all part of Sodeo.

Chorus

Follow me and to our places we'll go.
Now it's time for a story, you know.
Now the song is done and
We all know.
It's time for a story after Sodeo.

And that's the end of Sodeo.
Sit right down!

PART III

Family Storytimes

Songs and Stories for Everyone

Songs and stories are natural partners, as natural as songs and kids. And a natural atmosphere in which to share songs and stories with kids is one in which the children are surrounded by their brothers, sisters, parents, grandparents, aunts, or uncles. When families have an opportunity to listen to stories and enjoy songs together, it becomes a special event.

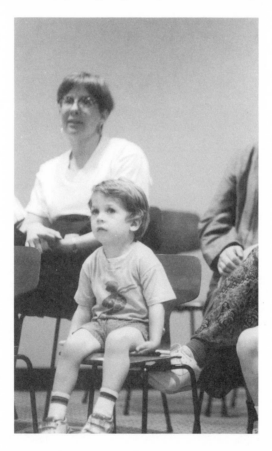

Children who are lucky enough to have parents, teachers, and librarians who read to them and share stories with them consider it a natural part of their lives. But sometimes, even those parents who actively read to their children may not get the chance to be part of an audience who can listen to stories and a family storytime allows them to share this experience. So for them, listening to stories and songs is a special treat for which they are an appreciative audience.

When they attend these programs, parents and other adults hear and appreciate again songs and stories they might have forgotten and are introduced to new songs and stories. As they share this experience with their children, the adults demonstrate how much they value stories, programs like this, and libraries. The use of songs as well as stories in your program lets this audience of parents and children participate together, listen together, share something together.

Songs Tell Their Own Stories

One of the compelling reasons to include songs in a Family Storytime at all is their unique place in American folk history. When children hear a song for the first time, it is wonderful for them. Thrilled with their discovery, they carry the song around with them, singing it over and over, enjoying their treasure. For you as a programmer, there is not only the joy of sharing in their discovery but also the realization that the child's "new" song has also entertained countless generations of children and adults.

Many of the songs included here are traditional folk songs, and as such, they tell a story of their own, quite apart from the story their lyrics tell. It's the story of the journey the songs have taken through history and the ways in which their words and meanings have changed as they wended their way through many countries, cultures, and generations of singers and listeners.

In their book *Folk Song U.S.A.* (Duell, Sloan & Pierce, 1947), John and Alan Lomax liken a folk song's growth to the sewing of a quilt: Old materials are sewn together to create new squares and, as each new square is added, a new quilt is created. Each time you sing one of these songs, you are adding your own squares to the quilt, expanding it, lengthening it, and deepening it as your own singing adds to the song's history.

Traditional songs have been sung in many ways, though there is only one version of each included in this book. You can find a different way to sing "The Fox" or "Frog Went a Courtin'" with every collection of children's songs you find. The words sung, the melodies used, the number of verses, even the characters' names can change, depending on where a particular song was sung and the people who sang it.

The Fox is always the hero of his song, portrayed in most versions not as a predator, but as just a hungry animal out on a chilly night to provide food for his family. But the variations on this song are endless. The names for the human characters range from "Old Mother Hippletoe" who spouts, "I think I heard her holler quing quarney-o," in a version collected from Texas to "Old Mother Slipper-Slopper" who calls out, "John, John, the grey goose is dead," in another version, with many variations in-between.

In the version of "Billy Boy" the Lomaxes included in their book, *Folk Songs, U.S.A.*, the hero, fresh from the American frontier, is courting a girl named Betsy Jane who is "tall as a pine and straight as a vine" who can "make a pair of breeches fast as you can count the stitches" and who is "fair, just touch her if you dare." Far different is the more sedate, widely known and sung variant included here, that has been traced to an older, British song in which the unnamed object of Billy's affection, although she can bake a cherry pie, is not a "young thing" at all but eighty-five years old.

On the American frontier, "play-party" songs evolved when strict (usually religious) tradition prevented dancing and the playing of instruments. Young people combined singing and movements like the choosing of partners and square-dance steps to invest this alternative form. "Skip to My Lou" is perhaps one of the best known of these songs. It has amassed hundreds of verses throughout its history. Some of them retain the flirtatiousness of boys and girls choosing partners, while others give a real flavor for frontier farming life with such lines as, "Cows in the cornfield, two by two," or "Rats in the bread-tray, how they chew." Still others begin to sound like the kind of game song it has now become: "Little red wagon, painted blue" and "Train is a-coming, choo, choo, choo."

Any traditional song will take strains from the various cultures through which it has traveled and these strains will echo again and again, no matter how many small changes the song may undergo. "Sodeo" is included here as a Preschooler song on page 82 and as a Family Storytime song on page 144, and each time, it is a different song. But its tune, rhythm, and repeating phrases, "to the front, to the back, to the seesaw side," echo the African-American line game, "Step Back, Sally," like the version found in *Shake It to the One That You Love the Best*, compiled by Cheryl Warren Mattox, (Warren-Mattox Productions, 1989). It's described as a line game that takes its singers "strutting down the alley," and singing "Step Back, Sally." Another version from the African-American tradition by way of the

Georgia Sea Islands is included in *Step It Down* by Bessie Jones and Bess Lomax Hawes (Harper & Row, 1972). In this variant everyone dances the "Zudie-O all night long." Yet another form of this song, from the *Raffi Singable Songbook* (Crown, 1980), takes its flavor from Canada, uses the song title of "Sodeo," and repeats the phrase "Step Back, Sally" but with another chant of its own.

Although newer songs may not have histories as long, rich, or varied as many of the traditional songs, it's worth the effort required to find out who wrote a particular song and why they wrote it. That knowledge can add its own special flavor to your program and the songs you sing will begin to tell their own stories, stories others will remember and spread. So sing the songs and acknowledge the people, cultures, and traditions from which they've sprung, both new and old. They will enhance and bring depth to your program and add to your audience's enjoyment.

Planning Your Program

A Family Storytime is an experience different from the traditional story-times aimed at a specific group of children—whether infants, preschoolers or school-aged children. A Family Storytime is an attempt to go past the traditional programming and bring parents and children together to share stories and songs in a comfortable atmosphere conducive to listening and sharing. In planning for and establishing a Family Storytime Program, keep both its concept and audience in mind.

Hopefully, a wide and varied assortment of ages will attend your program; but regardless, you'll need to think about and anticipate—at least to some extent—the ages of the children *likely* to attend. If you've been programming to preschoolers and toddlers for any length of time, many of your loyal preschooler fans will show up at your family storytimes no matter what minimum age you may have set. So as you select your stories and songs, keep that in mind. Sometimes, shorter participatory songs and stories can work well to charm little ones and entertain their older siblings and parents as well.

Try to find a time when the audience you want to reach will come in for your program. Sunday afternoons in winter can be a time when parents will gather up their children and come in to the library to listen to stories and songs. During the spring and especially summer, evening hours may be better for families, for as the weather warms up and the days lengthen, they may be more willing to venture out after supper than they might be during the shorter days of fall and winter.

One key to a successful program, other than the essential components of stories and songs, which will be discussed later, is to let your public know about the program you're planning. Expand your traditional avenues of publicity to reach your intended audience. Since you are trying to reach families with school-aged children, explore the possibility of sending publicity to the local schools, and your town's Recreation Department. The PTA may also be helpful in spreading the word. Be as clear as possible in your publicity to ensure your public knows what kind of program you're offering, and the intended audience, as well as the time and place.

As simple as it sounds, a successful program depends on choosing both songs and stories with which you are comfortable and which work well together. Use as many or as few songs in your program as you feel comfortable singing. And even if you start with only one song, that one small addition to your usual storytelling, or even to a picture-book program will create an event that everyone will enjoy. Almost forty Family Storytime songs are included here as well as suggestions for stories to tell. Let's take a look at the process of selecting and combining them into a workable and comfortable program.

Choosing Songs

New or old, traditional or original, the one element common to the following songs is their versatility; their lyrics and melodies make them ultimately singable and memorable. Even though many of the songs have several verses, not every verse needs to be sung. Some of these songs have been created or used for very specific occasions. But that doesn't mean they can't be enjoyed in a variety of circumstances.

So, how to choose? One of the things that led to the writing of this book was that very problem: what to sing and how to choose from among the hundreds of songs in the dozens of collections and recordings available. Even the thirty-nine songs collected here still require decisions about what to select and when to use them to best effect.

The same criteria that go into choosing a story to tell or a picture book to read can also be applied to the selection of a song. Sing the songs you like and that you feel comfortable singing. Choose those songs that you think will work well with the group to whom you will be programming. Although all of these songs have been used in different programs at one time or another and the audiences have enjoyed them, that's not to say that every song will fit every occasion or every audience.

If you are new to the idea of music in programs, you might consider coaxing other new singers to participate with call-and-response songs, such as the two included here, "John the Rabbit" and "Did You Go to the Barney?" Both can be sung or chanted and give your audience the flavor of a traditional storytelling technique. And what could be easier than "Bingo"? Familiar to children in every camp or school, it's a dog song that needs no introduction or accompaniment. "Do Your Ears Hang Low?" is so brief it has a history longer than the song itself. With ridiculous lyrics and the option to repeat its four lines as often as you wish, this is a song with enough silliness to make everyone smile and relax.

Soon, you'll be ready to sink your teeth into some longer songs. Try starting with songs like "I've Been Working on the Railroad" or "She'll Be Comin' Round the Mountain" (the latter is listed with the Preschooler songs), since you and your audience probably know them already and they will always elicit some response. But even songs like "New River Train" or "The Birds Song," which may not be as familiar to you, are still classic songs that will be easy to pick up for you and your audiences. Soon, they will be as familiar to you as the old favorites.

You may notice some identical titles in the Family Storytime songs and the Preschooler songs, but certain key elements about them change as they travel from one group to the other. Even though the traditional words to many of these songs can be used for any age group, from toddlers to grandparents, the singable, adaptable melodies of these songs also lend themselves to a bit of creativity. The version of "Skip To My Lou" that is included for Family Storytimes uses the traditional verses. For pre-schoolers, however, the words that precede the phrase "Skip to my Lou" are changed to simple action phrases like, "Clap your hands" or "Walk around."

In a Family Storytime, or with a group of older children, try doing "Skip To My Lou" as a round the way it's suggested on page 113. The idea of using songs in this way may seem a bit elaborate, especially with a group you do not know well. But people are usually surprisingly willing to try singing the song this way. And you will find that, despite some false starts or minor glitches, it will give your audience a unique way to participate, so that they remember and enjoy a traditional American song.

Both versions of "Sodeo" I have included, found in the Preschoolers' section on page 82 and in the Family Storytime Songs section on page 144, have taken a leap from the *original* traditional words, as discussed on page 89. But the song's traditional tune led easily to the writing of the equally silly lyrics that are part of the Family Storytime song. The small story they tell gives the audiences a chance to listen—and laugh—at the verses and join in with singing and moving for the chorus.

For the preschoolers, "Sodeo" underwent the same kind of transformation that was true for "Skip to My Lou." It has become a song about moving, turning and clapping, while retaining its traditional flavor of a circle game/dance in the chorus. None of these songs have changed so much that it would be impossible to recognize them. But their adaptability has been shown to full advantage, so they can be sung and enjoyed with as many people as possible.

Even though "Hey Dum Diddeley Dum" underwent no dramatic transformation from the Preschoolers Songs to the Family Songs group, your presentation and introduction might change somewhat in deference to the age of the group before you. Little ones probably need more of a chance to try those syllables out before they sing them. "She'll Be Comin' Round the Mountain" is another song that can travel easily between the two groups with little change. But a family program is the perfect time to sing this as a cumulative song, complete with sound effects and motions. Be prepared, however, for the audience will be sure to come up with verses, sound effects, and motions of their own.

If you consistently draw an audience with a rather young average age, you'll need to acknowledge that and be prepared with stories that even the youngest audience member will enjoy. The patience of preschoolers, even with adults with them, will not be as great as older children.

Participation Stories

One way to program to such an audience is to choose stories that involve your audience in some way. Some of these "participation stories" are amazingly versatile. While they can work very well with "graduates" of the preschooler programs—children from around four to six—they will charm older audiences as well. They can be matched with any number of the sing-along songs included here. After all, sing-along songs are really "participation songs." Stories that will be successful with younger audiences are included in the annotated list of suggested stories.

Many classic picture books can also be told as stories that give your audience an opportunity to participate. "The Three Billy Goats Gruff" allows everyone a chance to "trip, trap" over the bridge with the goats. Listeners can echo "Not I" with each of the hardworking hen's lazy friends in "The Little Red Hen." And with Wanda Gág's classic story, you'll soon have audiences chanting with you, "Hundreds of cats, thousands of cats, millions and billions and trillions of cats."

Sometimes stories can start as quiet picture books and become much more. *The Elephant in a Well* is a picture book by Marie Hall Ets, originally published in 1972. A charming story in picture-book form, it is quietly and very simply told. But it can be a storytelling experience as elaborate as the teller and audience want it to be. Marcia Lane, a New

York City-based storyteller, uses American Sign Language to enhance the story and give the audience a unique opportunity to participate. Each time a new animal is introduced in this cumulative tale, the audience is taught the sign for that animal. As the story unfolds, audiences join in with each animal's sign as all the animals try to pull the elephant out of the well. The use of the signs for each animal, and even for key words in the story like "help" or "pull" can make this a fun, lively, interactive story for everyone.

One evening, after I had spent the day in a local elementary school where I had told that story several times as I traveled through the classrooms, a little girl from the school saw me working at the library. She gave me a big smile and brought her father over to meet me. She started to tell her Dad, in English, that I was the lady who had visited her class that day. But since her Dad did not understand her, she started telling him in Spanish, her hands repeating some of the signs she had just learned from the story. So, of course, even though I don't speak Spanish, I knew just what she was saying. The special language of the story had done its job.

Another story with a particular emphasis on participation is a selection from *Joining In: An Anthology of Audience Participation Stories and How to Tell Them*, compiled by Teresa Miller (Yellow Moon Press, 1988). The collection contains eighteen stories that have been used by many well-known tellers, who have included their own suggestions for telling the stories as well as notes on sources and variants.

"The Lion and The Rabbit," from that collection, is a fable from India that has been adapted by storyteller Heather Forest. The participation element in this story is an "echo." The storyteller asks the listeners to be the lion's echo and gives them an opportunity to "roar" with all their hearts, souls—and voices. As they echo the lion's roar and his words, they are drawn into the story, and become a part of it. So, they remember it. And they remember its message about the small, but clever, rabbit who outwits the big, ferocious, self-centered, and not-too-bright lion.

Another way to program to audiences with younger children is to tell stories that involve some kind of visual stimulation, such as draw-and-tell stories or flannel boards. Flannel-board stories need not be just for preschoolers and some of the books listed in "Storytelling Resources" have good suggestions for visual stories that will entertain a broad age range.

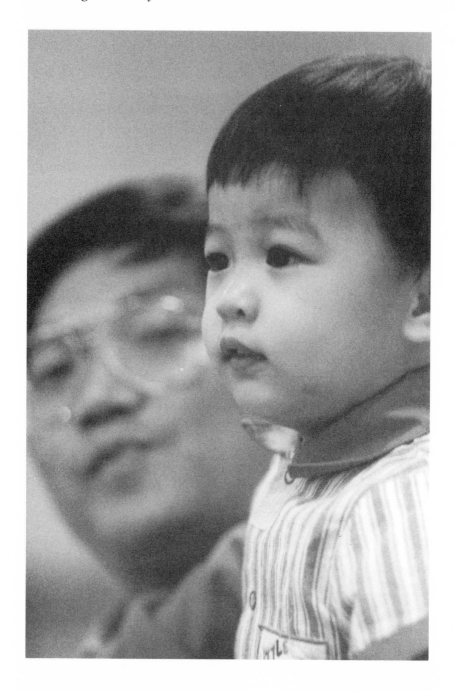

Other Story Ideas

As your efforts to reach those families with older children begin to pay off and your audiences become more diverse, you can introduce some longer stories into your programs. Many of them can incorporate some way for audiences to become part of the story. There may be a refrain that is repeated throughout a story, like the first-born son's name in "Tikki Tikki Tembo" or the magic words for the rock in "Anansi and the Moss Covered Rock" that they can pick up and repeat along with you. Some stories, like "Sody Salyratus" or "The Banza," have a melody or small song that can be sung a couple of times throughout the story. There may be an opportunity for audiences to clap their hands at certain times as the story unfolds, the way you can clap your hands with each of the characters in "The Vanishing Pumpkin." The very anticipation an audience feels as the story unfolds will become a part of the story and can affect your telling.

As long as you enjoy the story you are telling, your audiences will enjoy it too. Many of the collections listed in "Storytelling Resources" have a wide range of stories from which to choose, as well as tips on choosing, learning and telling a story effectively.

Program Ideas

As you go through the process of choosing songs to sing and stories to tell, you will discover that their universal appeal will provide you with an endless variety of ways to put them together in a program. There are, for example, many animal songs included here and they will be a good match for the animal stories that are also suggested. In fact, many of the animal songs and stories tell more than one tale! "Down By the Bay" is a song about animals, but it's also a silly song and a cumulative song. Its invitation to sing along makes it a perfect match for any of the silly, cumulative, participation stories that are also about animals, like "The Little Red Hen," "The Three Billy Goats Gruff," or "The Lion and the Rabbit."

"The Banza" is a story about a goat and a tiger, but it's also a story about friendship and trust and a story with a strong female character. "All God's Critters Got a Place in the Choir" is a song about animals, but it's also about friendship, sharing—and singing. In fact, some songs are so tailor-made for certain stories, it would be impossible to resist combining them. "So Long My Mom" on page 146, Bill Harley's interactive song that can be used with American Sign Language in the chorus and audience suggestions to build each verse, seems a perfect match for *The Elephant in A Well*, when that story is also told with American Sign Language.

Though the Halloween songs and stories seem to limit you to that time of year, there are some people who can't resist a scary story or song no matter what time of the year it is. And several of the songs may not seem seasonal, but can be perfect for holidays and occasions. "The Magic Penny Song" and "Frog Went A'Courtin" work well as Valentine songs but don't forget "Lavender's Blue" or "Billy Boy," two very different ways to look at love. "Douglas Mountain" is more than a lullaby. Its lyrics evoke the warmth of a fireside in winter and calm feeling of nighttime falling over everyone.

Celebrate the earth with "The Garden Song" or "All God's Critters," two songs that seem good complements for stories like "How Coyote Decorated the Night Sky" or "The Lion and the Rabbit." You might want to choose American folk songs like "Skip to My Lou", "The Fox," and "Sweet Betsy from Pike" to use with "Sody Sallyratus," an Appalachian tale and "We're Going on a Bear Hunt," another American story. Or take a trip around the world by singing songs like "The Story Song," which has its origins in a Jewish tale, "The Birds' Song," which goes back to England for its roots, and "So Long My Mom," which can take you on a trip anywhere you want to go. Tell stories from as many different countries as you want to use like China ("Tikki Tembo"), India ("The Lion and the Rabbit"), or Haiti ("The Banza").

Keep trying new selections and adding your favorites to the stories and songs contained here, so that even the number of combinations will continue to grow. Though storytimes don't need a theme to be successful, some kind of unifying thread running through the stories and songs gives the program its own shape and that makes it easier for you to balance its different elements. When you present a program as a unified whole that makes sense to you, it will make sense to your audience.

As you get to know more songs and different versions of traditional songs, you might prefer to sing about Mr. Rat, rather than Mr. Frog, who "goes a courtin'" or invent entirely new colors for "Jennie Jenkins" to wear—or reject! The verses for "Skip to My Lou" need not end with life on the prairie. New verses, for suburban and urban children of the nineties are yet to be sung—perhaps by you.

Even the songs being written, sung, and passed around today have begun to write histories of their own. Latter-day troubadours like Tom Paxton, Bill Harley, and Raffi write classic children's songs in the folk tradition with lively singable melodies shouting out for more and more verses to be invented for them. As all songs are sung, their melodies are being woven into history's fabric, making it stronger and more beautiful.

A few words here about the selection and presentation of the songs in this section. I chose a particular version because of its accessibility, and therefore, its singability. The melody line given, as well as the chords suggested, use keys that are, for the most part, mid-range and will fit a large number of voices. If you don't read music, check the list of recorded collections, as well. Many of the songs are on at least one of those tapes, so you can learn the song by listening to it.

If music and singing are familiar territory for you, you may have already used some of these songs at one time or another. But perhaps you will discover some new tunes or untried verses to add to your repertoire.

If you are new to singing, you are about to embark on an adventure that will add depth to your programs and give pleasure to your audiences. Remember, as you look through the songs suggested here, that many of them are short, easy, and recognizable enough to be used anywhere, at any time, by anyone. As you discover more and more of these songs and present them to a group, you are including the audience on your voyage of discovery. And they will enjoy it as much as you will. Sing, share, and listen with your heart, join in the chorus of voices rising and be part of music's power. Discover that songs do, indeed, tell a story.

PART IV

Family Storytime Songs

Song Categories

The songs in this section are a collection of vastly different selections gathered from a wide number of sources. They have been divided into flexible categories: Traditional American Songs, Favorites: Old and New, Silly Songs, Halloween Songs, and Lullabies. The categories have been supplied both to help you locate songs and to give some guidance when you put together a program. They are not intended to make any grand distinction between one song and another, since any good song is wonderfully adaptable. Many times, a particular song could fit easily into more than one category.

So, use the suggested categories only if they help you to remember the songs. Just take the songs, sing them, share them, and enjoy them.

These ten tunes are only a thin slice of the American heritage of songs. Some, like "Billy Boy" and "Jennie Jenkins," immigrated to America and have changed as they have become more and more a part of the American landscape. Others, like "I've Been Working on the Railroad" and "Sweet Betsy from Pike" are home grown. Try these as a taste of the wide variety of traditional American songs available and you'll see that they can add a delectable flavor to any program.

Call-and-response songs or chants can be used with any age group, especially with a group of parents and children of all ages. They involve an audience easily and call for no singing talent whatsoever for either performer or audience! Long rooted in the African-American tradition, call-and-response songs can work their way into many of your programs for both preschoolers and families. Here are two suggestions.

John the Rabbit

Until they get the hang of this, you can give your audience some kind of signal (thumbs up, hand claps, finger pointing) so they know when it's their turn to respond. Here the responses are in italics. Music is suggested, but chanting works just as well.

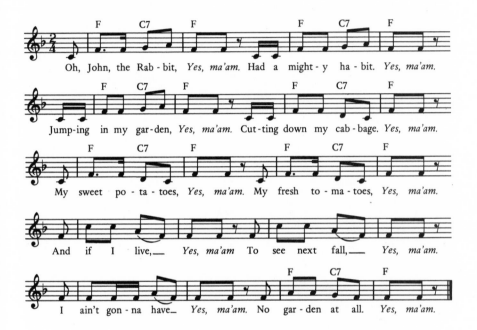

Did You Go to the Barney?

Although the original words for this next call-and-response song are rooted in a rural, farm context, they can be changed to suit an endless number of occasions. Instead of "Did you go to the barney?", you can ask "Did you go to the firehouse?", or "Did you go to your classroom?," or "Did you go to the zoo?", with children responding "Yes, ma'am." to the first question, with a second question like, "Did you climb on the fire-truck?" or "Did you ring the bell?" as some possibilities for other questions. The last question can be changed to suit the verse you're using, but whether you chant or sing this one, be sure that the last answer, whether it's "smooth" or any other adjective, is spoken.

Call-and-response begs for improvisation and fun and this song is sure recipe for that.

Billy Boy

Although the last verse of this song usually produces a laugh, there is an opportunity for everyone to participate in the song long before that point by using the last line of each verse, "She's a young thing and cannot leave her mother" as a sing-along. Although there are only a few verses included here, many other collections have several more verses, so re-search and add as many as you and your audience will enjoy.

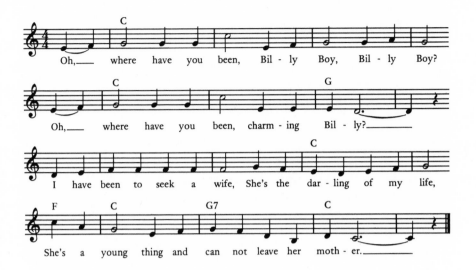

Oh,— where have you been, Bil - ly Boy, Bil - ly Boy?
Oh,— where have you been, charm - ing Bil - ly?—
I have been to seek a wife, She's the dar - ling of my life,
She's a young thing and can not leave her moth - er.—

Additional verses:

Did she bid you to come in, Billy Boy, Billy Boy?
Did she bid you to come, charming Billy?
Yes, she bade me to come in,
There's a dimple on her chin,
She's a young thing and cannot leave her mother.

Can she bake a cherry pie, Billy Boy, Billy Boy?
Can she bake a cherry pie, charming Billy?
She can bake a cherry pie
In the twinkling of an eye
She's a young thing and cannot leave her mother.

How old is she, Billy Boy, Billy Boy?
How old is she, charming Billy?
She is three times six four times seven,
Twenty eight and eleven.
She's a young thing and cannot leave her mother!

I've Been Working on the Railroad

This makes a great singalong as everyone knows the words.

I've been work-ing on the rail-road All the live-long day,

I've been work-ing on the rail-road Just to pass the time a - way.

Don't you hear the whis-tle blow-ing? Rise up so ear-ly in the morn.

Don't you hear the cap-tain shout-ing, "Di - nah, blow your horn"?

Di - nah, won't you blow, Di - nah, won't you blow,

Di - nah, won't you blow your horn?___ Di - nah, won't you blow,

Di - nah, won't you blow, Di - nah, won't you blow your horn?

Some-one's in the kit-chen with Di - nah, Some-one's in the kit-chen I

know,_____ Some-one's in the kit-chen with Di - nah,

Strum-min' on the old ban - jo. (He's strum-min') Fee - fi

fid - dle - e - i - o,   fee - fi   fid - dle - e - i - o,____

Fee - fi   fid - dle - e - i - o!   Strum - min' on   the   old   ban - jo.

Skip to My Lou

If you have two people leading a program, you can also try this song as a round. Divide your audience in half. Lead one side of the room in singing the chorus, while the other group sings a verse. The easy rhythm of the song is as clear whether you are singing the verses or the chorus. So, while one side of the aisle sings, "Lost my partner, what'll I do?" the other sings, "Skip, skip, skip to my Lou." With a little practice, it will work fine.

Skip,   skip,   skip   to   my   Lou,   Skip,   skip,   skip   to   my   Lou,

Skip,   skip,   skip   to   my   Lou,   Skip   to   my   Lou,   my   dar - ling.

Lost   my   part - ner,   what'll   I   do?   Lost   my   part - ner,   what'll   I   do?

Lost   my   part - ner,   what'll   I   do?   Skip   to   my   Lou,   my   dar - ling.

Additional verse:

I'll get another one prettier than you. . .
Skip to my Lou, my darling.

Chorus

Fly in the buttermilk, shoo fly shoo. . .
Skip to my Lou, my darling.

The Fox

Long a popular song, with many versions in various collections, this next song is one that is still fun to sing. The pictures it paints—the captive ducks and geese being carted away, "their legs all dangling down-o" and "Old Mother Pitter-Patter" calling for her man John to take his revenge while Papa Fox's little ones are enjoying a fine supper—will spark imaginations. The last two lines of each verse, which are repetitions of earlier lines, present opportunities for singing along.

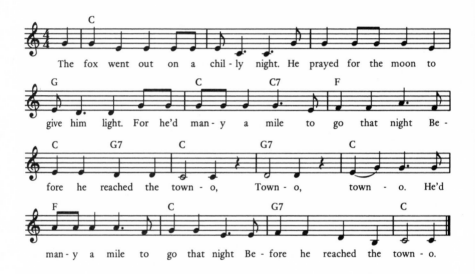

He ran till he came to a great big bin,
The ducks and the geese were put therein.
Said, "A couple of you will grease my chin
Before I leave this town-o.
Town-o, town-o.
A couple of you will grease my chin
Before I leave this town-o.

He grabbed the gray goose by the neck,
Slung the little one down over his back,
He didn't mind at all their quack, quack, quack,
And their legs all dangling down-o.
Down-o, down-o.
He didn't mind at all their quack, quack, quack,
And their legs all dangling down-o.

Old Mother Pitter-Patter jumped out of bed.
Out of the window she cocked her head,
Crying, "John, John, the gray goose is gone
And the fox is on the town-o,
Town-o, town-o.
Crying, "John, John, the gray goose is gone
And the fox is on the town-o.

John he went to the top of the hill,
Blew on his horn both loud and shrill,
The fox, he said, "I better flee with my kill,
He'll soon be on my trail-o, trail-o, trail-o."
The fox he said, "I'd better flee with my kill,
He'll soon be on my trail-o.

He ran till he came to his cozy den,
There were the little ones, eight, nine, ten.
They said, "Daddy, you better go right back again,
Cause it must be a might fine town-o,
Town-o, town-o."
They said, "Daddy, you better go right back again.
Cause it must be a might fine town-o."

Then the fox and his wife without any strife,
They cut up the goose with a fork and knife.
They never had such a fine supper in their life.
And the little ones chewed on the bones-o,
Bones-o, bones-o.
They never had such a supper in their life.
And the little ones chewed on the bones-o.

Frog Went A-Courtin'

The saga of the frog has many different versions and could go on for hours, depending on the song in which you find him. One version from Virginia that was collected by Ruth Seeger in *American Folk Songs for Children* (Doubleday & Co., 1948), lasts for twenty verses. In that one, Miss Mouse, when asked in marriage by Mr. Frog, asks for Uncle Rat's consent, they plan the wedding, and then recount the guest list and the festivities. Nancy and John Langstaff, in *Jim Along Josie* (Harcourt, Brace, Jovanovich, Inc., 1970), have found an "Appalachian Mountain Tune" in which it takes twenty-five verses to relate the tale of courtship, wedding, and guests. And in *Ring Around the Moon* by Edith Fowke (Prentice-Hall, 1977), it is Mr. Rat, rather than Mr. Frog, who comes to court Miss Mouse. In the version I've chosen, only the barest elements of the plot appear. Since the song is familiar to so many people, you probably won't have trouble encouraging your audience to join in for the whole song. But, for those in your group who aren't as willing—or as sure of the words or tune—the "hm-hm's" provide a handy spot for them to join in.

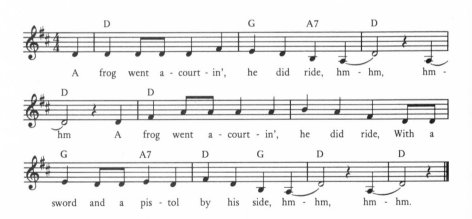

He rode up to Miss Mousie's den (hm-hm, hm-hm)
He rode up to Miss Mouse's den
Said "Please Miss Mousie, won't you let me come in" (hm-hm, hm-hm)

"Yes, Sir Frog, I sit and spin." (hm-hm, hm-hm)
"Yes, Sir Frog, I sit and spin,
Please, Mr. Froggie, won't you come right in" (hm-hm, hm-hm)

Frog said, "My dear, I've come to see," (hm-hm, hm-hm)
Frog said, "My dear, I've come to see,
If you, Miss Mousie, will marry me." (hm-hm, hm-hm)

"Without my Uncle Rat's consent, (hm-hm, hm-hm)
Without my Uncle Rat's consent,
I would not marry the president!" (hm-hm, hm-hm)

Uncle Rat gave his consent, (hm-hm, hm-hm)
Uncle Rat gave his consent,
That they should marry and be content, (hm-hm, hm-hm)

"Oh, yes, Sir Frog, I'll marry you. (hm-hm, hm-hm)
Oh, yes, Sir Frog, I'll marry you,
And we'll have children two by two." (hm-hm, hm-hm)

The frog and the mouse they went to France, (hm-hm, hm-hm)
The frog and the mouse they went to France
And that's the end of my romance. (hm-hm, hm-hm)

Frog's bridle and saddle are laid on the shelf, (hm-hm, hm-hm)
Frog's bridle and saddle are laid on the shelf,
If you want any more, you must sing it yourself! (hm-hm, hm-hm)

Sweet Betsy from Pike

An appealing mixture of pathos and humor and the opportunity to join in with a few "hoodle-dangs" will make this fun for everybody.

One evening quite early they camped on the Platte.
'Twas near by the road on a green shady flat.
Where Betsy, sorefooted, lay down to repose,
With wonder Ike gazed on his Pike County rose.

Chorus

The Shanghai ran off, and their cattle all died.
That morning the last piece of bacon was fried.
Poor Ike was discouraged and Betsy got mad.
The dog drooped his tail and looked wondrously sad.

Chorus

They soon reached the desert where Betsy gave out,
And down in the sand she lay rolling about.

While Ike half distracted looked on with surprise.
Saying, "Betsy, get up, you'll get sand in your eyes."

Chorus

Sweet Betsy got up in a great deal of pain.
Declared she'd go back to Pike County again.
But Ike gave a sigh, and they fondly embraced,
And they traveled along with his arm round her waist.

Chorus

Riddle Song

The combination of riddling and gift-giving to one's love makes this an
apt choice for storytelling programs—about love, or gifts, or riddles.

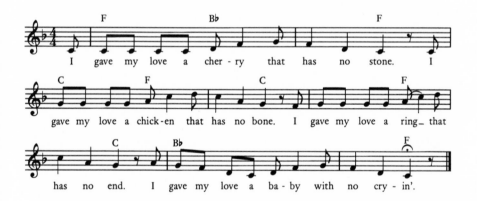

How can there be a cherry that has no stone?
How can there be a chicken that has no bone?
How can there be a ring that has no end?
How can there be a baby with no crying?

A cherry when it's bloomin', it has no stone.
A chicken when it's pippin', it has no bone.
A ring when it's rollin', it has no end.
A baby when it's sleepin', there's no cryin'.

Jennie Jenkins

In its evolution, this song has gone from elaborate ritual to answer-back song to nonsense song. In its present form, it is still a favorite and appears in countless collections of songs for children.

All about that flirtatious and contrary heroine, Jennie, this can work well as a call-and-response song with a number of different variations. If two people are leading the program, one can answer the questions while the other responds. If you are the only leader, however, your group can ask the questions—after a brief period of instruction and practice—and you can respond. About the chorus: it really is a tongue twister and will be fun to sing once your audience has gotten the hang of it. Go over it several times—slowly—before you start. It'll save a lot of frustration and twisted tongues.

Additional verses:

Oh, will you wear green, oh my dear, oh my dear?
Oh, will you wear green, Jennie Jenkins.
No, I won't wear green, I'm ashamed to be seen.

Chorus

    Oh, will you wear white. . .
    It don't suit me right. . .

Chorus

    Oh, will you wear yeller. . .
    It wont get me no feller. . .

Chorus

    Oh, will you wear red. . .
    It's the color of my head. .

Although these songs are vastly different from one another, they will soon become some of your favorites with their appealing melodies and lyrics. From a love ballad like "The Birds Song" to every child's choice, "Puff, the Magic Dragon," the appeal of these songs will soon become evident.

The Birds' Song

"The Birds' Song," also called the "Leatherwing Bat" in some collections, can be found in several music books for children. Some parts of the song have been traced to Chaucer's *Parliament of Foules*, a long poem written in rhyme-royale, probably between 1372 and 1386.

Five different birds sing their lament in this song and although the chorus uses nonsense words, it has a plaintive melody that adds to the troubadour quality of the song and gives your audience an opportunity to participate and still listen to the small drama that unfolds in each verse.

"Ho," said the little leather-winged bat,
"I'll tell you the reason that,
The reason that I fly at night
Is 'cause I've lost my heart's delight."

Chorus

"Hi," said the woodpecker sittin' on the fence.
"Once I courted a handsome wench.
She proved fickle and from me fled,
And ever since my head's been red."

Chorus

"Hi!" said the blue-bird as he flew,
"Once I loved a young gal, too,
But she got saucy and wanted to go,
So I bought me a new string for my bow."

Chorus

"Hi!" says the robin as he flew,
"When I was a young man, I choosed two.
If one didn't love me, the other one would,
And don't you think my notion's good?"

Chorus

New River Train

Another classic folk song, with repetitive words and a cumulative set of verses. In this case, it's numbers that accumulate. It can fit nicely into many programs, combined with "I've Been Working on the Railroad" or many of the other "love" songs.

Leav-ing on that New Riv-er train.   Leav-ing on that New Riv-er train.

It's the same old train that brought me here. And gon-na take me back a - gain.

Darling, you can't love but one
Darling, you can't love but one
Can't love but one and have any fun.
No, Darling you can't love but one.

Chorus

Darling, you can't love but two . . .
You can't love but two and your heart be true . . .

Chorus

Darling, your can't love but three. . .
You can't love but three and keep your love of me. . .

Chorus

Darling, you can't love but four. . .
You can't love but four and love me any more. . .

Chorus

Darling, you can't love but five. . .
You can't love but five and keep our love alive. . .

Chorus

I Had an Old Coat

This song has as many versions as it does verses. It appears in story form in Nancy Schimmel's *Just Enough To Make a Story* and adaptations of this basic idea have appeared in a few picture books. When singer/storyteller Marcia Lane sings this song in concert, she involves her audience in two ways. She invites them to sing the second "what'll I do" each time it repeats in a line. Then she intersperses the verses with a running commentary on the song, involving the audience in remembering all the forms the coat has taken in its journey from coat to song. It's about saving and reusing, but mostly it's fun.

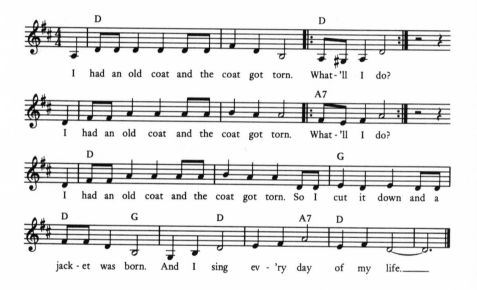

In a couple of years, those threads got thin.
What'll I do, what'll I do?
In a couple of years, those threads got thin.
What'll I do, what'll I do?
In a couple of years, those threads got thin.
So I called it a shirt and I tucked it in.
And I sing every day of my life.

Then the arms wore out in the east and west.
What'll I do, what'll I do?
Then the arms wore out in the east and west.
What'll I do, what'll I do?
Then the arms wore out in the east and west.
So I pulled them off and I had a vest.
And I sing every day of my life.

But the vest got stained with cherry pie.
What'll I do, what'll I do?
But the vest got stained with cherry pie.
What'll I do, what'll I do?
But the vest got stained with cherry pie.
So I cut and I sewed till I had a tie.
And I sing every day of my life.

But soon that tie was looking lean.
What'll I do, What'll I do?
But soon that tie was looking lean.
What'll I do, What'll I do?
But soon that tie was looking lean.
So I made it a patch for my old blue jeans.
And I sing every day of my life.

But soon that patch was almost gone.
What'll I do, What'll I do?
But soon that patch was almost gone.
What'll I do, What'll I do?
But soon that patch was almost gone.
With what was left I made this song,
That I sing every day of my life.

And I sing everyday of my life.

Garden Song

This song celebrates spring, gardens, nature and, in its most elemental form, digging in dirt. Written by David Mallett, sung by everyone from Pete Seeger to nursery school teachers, it can fit into many programs. The singable melody and simple opening words invite participation from all ages. With an audience who is unfamiliar with this song try singing only one of the verses or just the chorus at first.

Chorus

Plant your rows straight and long.
Season with a prayer and song.
Mother earth will make you strong,
If you give her loving care.
Old crow watching from a tree.
He's got his hungry eye on me.
In my garden I'm as free
As that feathered thief up there.

Puff, The Magic Dragon

Peter, Paul and Mary started singing this song thirty years ago and it hasn't lost any of its enormous popularity—for all ages! A little girl who was about three years old came faithfully to Preschool Songs and Stories every week. And every week, she asked for Puff. She always sang all the other songs but she always asked for Puff. So here it is.

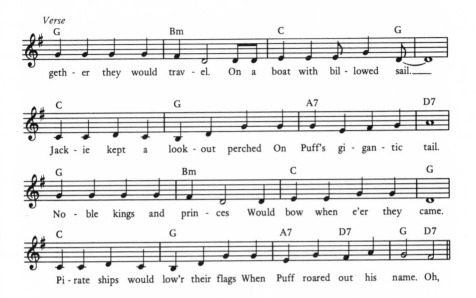

Verse

geth - er they would trav - el. On a boat with bil - lowed sail.___

Jack - ie kept a look - out perched On Puff's gi - gan - tic tail.

No - ble kings and prin - ces Would bow when e'er they came.

Pi - rate ships would low'r their flags When Puff roared out his name. Oh,

Dragons live forever.
But not so little boys.
Painted wings and giant's rings
Make way for other toys.
One grey night it happened,
Jackie Paper came no more.
And Puff that mighty dragon,
He ceased his fearless roar.

His head was bent in sorrow.
Green scales fell like rain.
Puff no longer went to play
Along the cherry lane.
Without his lifelong friend,
Puff could not be brave.
So Puff that mighty dragon
Sadly slipped into his cave.

Chorus

All God's Critters Got a Place In the Choir

Bill Staines's romp through the animal kingdom tells a story that will set hands to clapping and feet to stamping. It's a perfect blend of sing-along and storytelling. The chorus is easy to remember and the verses will take you through a roster of all creatures small and big, low and high, soft and loud.

The dogs and the cats they take up the middle
While the honeybee hums and the cricket fiddles
The donkey brays and the pony neighs
and the old coyote howls.

Chorus

Listen to the top where the little birds sing
On the melodies with the high notes ringing.
the hoot owl hollers over everything
And the jaybird disagrees.

Singing in the nighttime, singing in the day
The little duck quacks, then he's on his way.
The possum ain't got much to say.
and the porcupine talks to himself.

Chorus

It's a simple song of living sung everywhere
By the ox and the fox and the grizzly bear,
The grumpy alligator and the hawk above,
The sly raccoon and the turtle dove.

Chorus (2X)

Canoer's Lullaby

Cathy Winter, a singer, songwriter, and resident of New York State, was inspired to write this during an historic re-enactment of a canoe trip from Canada down the Hudson River into the Albany area in which New Yorkers, French Canadians, and Mohawk all participated. The chant in the song recalls the chants used by the Mohawk, whose actual tribal name is "Kaniengehaga" or "People of the Place of the Flint," to help them keep rhythm while paddling the canoe.

The chant becomes a call-and-response to establish your own rhythm. The verses and chorus use the melody shown for the first verse.

Chorus

> Won't you bring me the waters from Lac St. Louis
> That rush down the rapids just outside Lachine
> Go up the Richelieu into great Lake Champlain
> Past Height of Land to where the Hudson's been tamed.

Additional verses:

> The paddlers are sleeping,
> Their hearts so at ease
> To travel these waters in such fine company
> Later their arms will burn brown in the sun
> Hands to the paddles and moving as one.

Chorus

> Hills rise like dream sites
> Farms roll to view
> The fog starts to life,
> And the sun it shines through
> Waters from Canada, through Mohawk Lands
> Carried to my home by so many hands.

Chorus

> The route is an old one
> Many ancestors learned
> The boats, they were built
> by the hand at the stern
> Strong arm on young shoulder
> And smile on dark face
> Songs in the moonlight,
> And we all keep the pace.

Chant

Magic Penny

Over thirty years ago, in 1963, Malvina Reynolds published an anthology of songs called *Little Boxes and Other Handmade Songs* (Oak Publications). It is a small but powerful collection that includes songs that celebrate the earth and rail against its pollution; songs that celebrate people and protest hatred, and songs about bedtime, animals, and family that touch children's hearts. This song is the first to appear in that book. It is a song about giving and sharing that can set a perfect tone for many different kinds of programs.

Love is some-thing if you give it a-way, give it a way, give it a way.

Love is some-thing if you give it a-way, You'll end up hav-ing more.

It's just like a mag-ic pen-ny. Hold on tight and you won't have an-y.

Lend 'n spend it and you'll have so man-y, They'll roll all o-ver the floor. For

more. So let's go danc-ing 'til the break of day, And if there's a pi-per

we can pay. For love is some-thing if you give it a-way, You'll end up hav-ing more.

Additional verse:

> Money's dandy and we like to use it,
> But love is better if you don't refuse it.
> It's a treasure and you'll never lose it
> Unless you lock up your door, for. . .

Chorus

Coda:

> Let's go dance until the break of day.
> If there's a piper, we can pay.
> Cause love is something if you give it away,
> You'll end up having more.

You'll Sing a Song and I'll Sing a Song

Ella Jenkins' classic invitation to sing, hum, or whistle along will be sure to be enjoyed by everyone—even those who think they don't want to sing. It's perfect to use as a program opener or anywhere as a pace change with longer songs or stories.

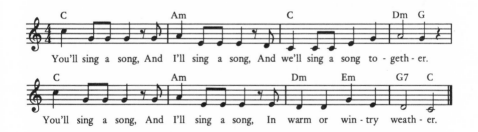

C   Am   C   Dm G

You'll sing a song, And I'll sing a song, And we'll sing a song to - geth - er.

C   Am   Dm   Em   G7 C

You'll sing a song, And I'll sing a song, In warm or win - try weath - er.

Additional verses:

> You'll play a tune, and I'll play a tune. . .

> You'll whistle a tune, and I'll whistle a tune. . .

Precious Friends

Written by Pete Seeger in 1974, this song celebrates peace, harmony, and friendship. It has no chorus geared to singing along. It has no repeating phrase that can be picked up easily. But it does have the unique style and sentiment that are part of any Pete Seeger song and can be a lovely choice to end your program. Unless you provide copies of the words, you'll have to sing it alone the first time. But, on the second singing, you'll have some precious new friends to sing along with you.

Here are a half-dozen ways to get your group laughing and singing. "Bingo" and "Do Your Ears Hang Low" are two short, sweet, well-known songs that can plug any hole in a program. Use them after a long story when your group's listening powers have been put to the test or between two shorter stories. Then, three songs sing about animals in all manner of improbable guises and disguises. And last, but not least, comes a refrain all parents usually dread, but here it becomes a spoof with endless verses to be invented—depending on what's happening that day.

Bingo

This is a perennial favorite most of your audience will know well and will join in singing enthusiastically. With each successive verse, the first letter is dropped off and a clap replaces the letter. Then the second, the third and so on until the refrain is all clapping.

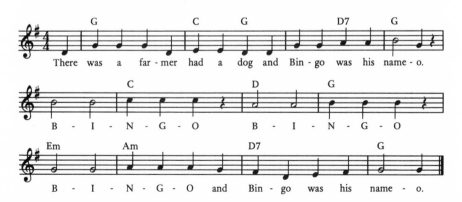

Do Your Ears Hang Low

This silly song dates back to the American Revolution as the reference to the soldiers indicates. It invites dramatic improvisation as you let ears hang low, wobble them and so on. It's short and can fill in anywhere or you can lengthen it by singing it over . . . and over . . . and over.

Do your ears hang low, do they wob - ble to and fro?
Can you tie them in a knot, can you tie them in a bow?
Can you fling them o - ver your shoul - der
Like a Con - ti - nen - tal sol - dier, Do your ears hang low?

If I Had a Dinosaur

Raffi's instinctive talent for writing songs that kids will like and remember is evident in this selection. Dinosaurs still enjoy enormous popularity with the preschool and kindergarten crowd, so use this song to spark young imaginations and send them on flights of fancy. Raffi did not write the last two verses—but if you work in a library, they are fun to add.

The best way to make this an effective sing-along is to sing the last line of each verse twice so your audience can join in the second time.

And If I had a dinosaur, just think what we could see.
We could look inside the cloud above my balcony.

And If I had a dinosaur, just think where we could go.
All the way to Grandma's house, to play her piano.

And If I want a dinosaur, I know just where I'd look.
I'd run right to the library and look into a book.

There I'd have a dinosaur, or maybe five or six.
Steropods, Triceratops, Tyranosaurus Rex.

Down by the Bay

A song that has been popular in various guises since World War I, this is adaptable to a range of styles. For instance, each phrase you sing can be repeated by the audience as an echo: "Down by the bay (Down by the bay)/Where the watermelons grow (Where the watermelons grow)." Or, you can save the sing-along aspect for the chorus, inviting your audience to sing each silly question after you sing it: "Did you ever see. . .? (Did you ever see. . . ?)" You can make it cumulative by singing the previous questions(s) before adding the newest one. If you try to use all of these suggestions in the same program, however, you might be in for a really long song!

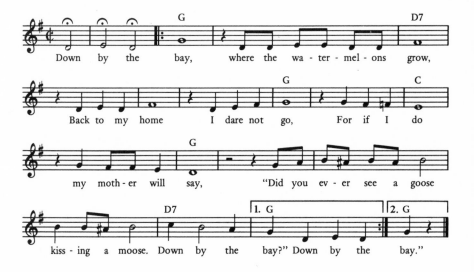

Additional verses:

Did you ever see a bee with a sunburned knee?
(Did you ever see a bee with a sunburned knee?)
Down by the bay?

Sing chorus before each new question, then sing previous question(s) before adding the new one.

Did you ever see a cow with a green eyebrow? . . .

Did you ever see a moose with a loose tooth? . . .

Did you ever see a witch digging a ditch? . . .

Did you ever see a whale with a polka dot tail? . . .

Did you ever see a fly wearing a tie? . . .

Did you ever see a bear combing his hair? . . .

Did you ever see llamas eating their pajamas? . . .

Down by the bay?

No matter how many refrains you tag on to your song, this last verse is always a good way to close. An added boon is that your audience will know it's the end of the song.

Down by the bay,
Where the watermelons grow
Back to my home,
it's time to go
And when I do
to my mother I'll say:

It's been going on too long, so let's end the song
Down by the bay.

Sodeo

Although this is a traditional song, these verses are new. They were written for a program that had nothing but "silly" songs and stories, but they could be used any time you need a silly song—or even a song about animals. A version of this song that concentrates more on movement and actions appears with the preschooler songs.

Additional verses:

I went to the store and you'll never guess:
I saw a dinosaur trying on a dress.
She was very mad because it wouldn't fit.
But I don't think they make size two hundred and six.

Chorus

> When I came home, what a shock it was!
> In my yard was a hippopotamus.
> She was very sad, a little frightened too.
> She said, "Can you bring me back to the zoo?"

Chorus 2X

I'm Gonna Tell

This song has been woven into the fabric of oral tradition, as each singer who uses it says, "I heard it from. . . ." Well, *I* heard it from Barre Tolkein, a folklorist and balladeer from Utah, who introduced the song by saying he had heard it from a friend. It turns one of the phrases parents dread most into a song that begs for new verses to be invented.

Chorus:

> I'm gonna tell that you took my ball.
> I'm gonna tell that you made me fall.
> I'll take back my Barbie and my coloring book, too.
> I'm gonna tell on you.

Chorus

> I'm gonna tell that you made me trip.
> That's why I scraped my knee and bit my lip.
> But you better not tell what I did to you.
> I'm gonna tell on you.

Chorus

So Long, My Mom

The first time I heard this next song Bill Harley, a nationally known singer, songwriter, and storyteller, sang it at the annual Hudson River Revival, a folk and storytelling festival in Westchester County, New York. Almost as an afterthought, he pointed to the signer who was there to interpret for the deaf and hearing impaired and decided to integrate sign language into the song. So, he taught us the signs for the chorus of the song.

This was, he explained, a traveling song. So, he needed to have people (meaning kids) in the audience tell him where they'd like to go, how they'd like to travel there and what they'd like to see when they got there. So it became a song we made up as we went along. And it will become different for you every time you use it. The best part is: everything works.

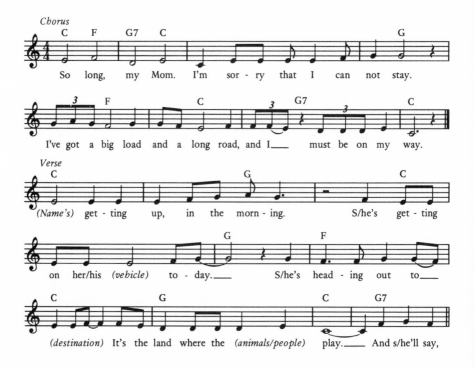

Since this a make-your-own-song, here's a verse with everything completed to give you an idea.

Dorothy's getting up in the morning.
She's getting on her skateboard today.
She's heading out to Arizona.
It's the land where the lizards play.
And she'll say:

Chorus

Hey Dum Diddeley Dum

A perfect choice for an opener, this song will break the ice and get even the shyest member of the audience involved. The easy, nonsense words of the chorus will be remembered long after the program.

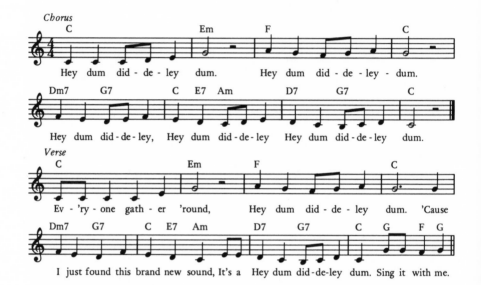

Chorus

> Come join in the fun,
> With a hey dum diddeley dum,
> We're gonna sing till the day is done,
> Hey dum diddeley dum.
> (Now it's your turn)

Chorus

> Everyone come and sing,
> With a hey dum diddeley dum.
> We're gonna make these rafters ring
> With our Hey dum diddeley dum.
> (sing it with me)

Chorus 2x

Of all the holidays, Halloween seems to be the most popular choice to celebrate with stories and songs. Spooky tales, silly ghosts, fat pumpkins, and clattering skeletons populate many a classroom, auditorium, and library story room every October as children sit transfixed, savoring every deliciously shivery minute.

The songs included here are a combination of the traditional, the improvisational and, yes, the silly. But they will yield a witch's brew that your whole storytime crowd will love.

Halloween's Here

The first song, to the tune of "Mister Sun" (p. 60), is a celebration of the things kids like best about Halloween—dressing up in costumes and trick-or-treating. The chorus is the time for everyone to sing along, so if you sing it twice at the beginning everyone will get used to it.

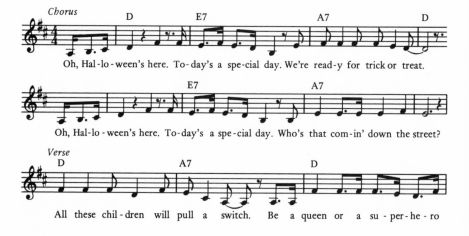

Oh, Hal-lo-ween's here. To-day's a spe-cial day. We're read-y for trick or treat.

Oh, Hal-lo-ween's here. To-day's a spe-cial day. Who's that com-in' down the street?

All these chil-dren will pull a switch. Be a queen or a su-per-he-ro

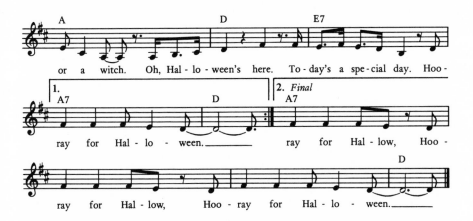

or a witch. Oh, Hal - lo - ween's here. To - day's a spe - cial day. Hoo -

ray for Hal - lo - ween.____ ray for Hal - low, Hoo -

ray for Hal - low, Hoo - ray for Hal - lo - ween.____

Chorus

We'll spook and scare you,
But just for fun.
So please give us treats
When all our spookin's done!
Oh, Halloween's here.
Today's a special day.
Hooray for Halloween.

Chorus

Ghosts and goblins are everywhere.
A special magic is in the air.
Oh Halloween's here.
Today's a special day.
(Last time only:)
Hooray for Hallow, hooray for Hallow,
Hooray for Halloween.

Five Little Pumpkins

This song is also on page 52 with the preschoolers' songs with directions for appropriate hand motions which can, of course, be included for any age group. But no matter how old your audience, this will be a hit. It seems nobody ever gets tired of singing about those five pumpkins.

Five lit-tle pump-kins sit-ting on a gate. The first one said, "Oh my, it's get-ting late." The sec-ond one said, "There are witch-es in the air." The third one said, "But I don't care." The fourth one said, "Let's run and run and run." The fifth one said, "I'm read-y for some fun." Oo - oo, went the wind and out went the light. And the five lit-tle pump-kins rolled out of sight.

Skeleton Bones

This song also works as a chant, picking up speed with each verse. Beat out the rhythm on the chorus by alternately clapping hands and slapping thighs, until, on the last line of the chorus, you stretch out the last "oh," raise your hands high and clap out a beat before "goodness they scare." On each verse, tap each bone as it's mentioned and keep the rhythm you've started in the chorus. Once your group has gotten the hang of it, go a bit faster on each verse until the last chorus is as fast as you can make it. This song might not be anatomically correct, but nobody will care.

With the hand bone connected to the wrist bone,
And the wrist bone connected to the arm bone,
And the arm bone connected to the shoulder bone,
Oh, goodness they scare!

Chorus

With the head bone connected to the neck bone,
And the neck bone connected to the shoulder bone,
And the shoulder bone connected to the back bone,
Oh, goodness they scare!

Chorus

Whippily, Whoppily, Whoop

This is an improvisational song in which the names of the singers, audience members, or local sites can be inserted into the various verses, as you can see by the place names used here. Your audience will be delighted with hearing familiar scenes mentioned in the song while they giggle at the thought of witches riding or goblins crawling down their local streets. Although the format here has one group leader, it can be done with two people as well; the leaders tell each other what they saw and what happened. But no matter how many people lead the song, the audience can join in on the "whippily, whoppily, whoop" s. It's a fun phrase to roll over your tongue so practice it a few times before you start to get them warmed up and ready.

Where are you witches a-going,
A-going, a-going?
Where are you witches a-going?
Whippily, whoppily, WHOOP.

We're going over to Anne's house,
To Anne's house, to Anne's house.
We're going over to Anne's house,
Whippily whoppily, WHOOP!

Why would you want to do that?
To do that, to do that?
Why would you want to do that?
Whippily, whoppily, WHOOP!

We're going trick or treating,
Or treating, or treating.
We're going trick or treating.
Whippily, whoppily, WHOOP!

This idea can be used for a whole cast of spooky characters: three monsters a'crawling, three ghosts a'flying, etc. They can be going to different people's houses, to the library, etc., to spook, to scare, or maybe because they want to hear a story.

What'cha Gonna Be For Halloween?

Here is an improvisational, interactive song, in which various audience members are asked what they're going to be for Halloween and a verse is sung about each in turn. This is a good song to end a program. More than once, though, I've found myself listening to all those children who were not picked to be in the song (due to time limitations) tell me what they were going to be for Halloween. That is, in fact, its only danger: you may find this song takes far longer than you had ever planned.

Chorus:

> Laura will be a princess for Halloween,
> For Halloween, for Halloween.
> Laura will be a princess for Halloween,
> For Halloween this year.
>
> Paul will be a monster for Halloween,
> For Halloween, for Halloween.
> Paul will be a monster for Halloween,
> For Halloween this year.

(Of course, some quick singing will be needed when a long name like "Stephanie" or "Demetrius" is paired with a character with an equally long name. Don't worry though: your audience will understand.)

Lullabies

Here is just a small selection from among many lullabies that can be popular and effective at storytime. Lullabies have a remarkably calming effect on a group of children and parents. There's lots of lap sitting, leaning, and hugging. Although it works nicely as a closing song, you don't have to save a lullaby for the end of a program. In the midst of other, lively pieces, it may gather back wandering minds, draw the group together, and get everyone more in the mood to listen. Of the six lullabies included, it seems that everyone knows "All the Pretty Little Horses" and "Lavender's Blue." But try some of the others, as well. They all are soft and gentle and can fit into a variety of programs. So remember that lullabies aren't just for the nursery or for bedtime.

All the Pretty Little Horses

A classic among lullabies, this draws its roots from the South, and the arrangement, words, and singing style of this song can vary greatly. But the sentiments of love and security for a baby who is going to sleep remain the same.

Lavender's Blue

Many collectors point to the nonsense words, "dilly dilly," and the pretend game that this song's words play. And, each version you find seems to contain some variations in the lyrics, especially in the second verse. But for me, the true sentiment and the real reason for singing this song are in its last verse and the words, "If you will love me . . . I will love you."

Lav - en - der's blue, dil - ly dil - ly, Lav - en - der's green. When I am king, dil - ly dil - ly, You shall be queen. Who told you so, dil - ly dil - ly, Who told you so? 'Twas my own heart, dil - ly dil - ly, That told me so. That told me so. 'Twas my own heart, dil - ly dil - ly, That told me so.

Call up my maids, dilly dilly,
At four o'clock.
Come to the wheel, dilly dilly,
And some to the rock.
Some to make hay, dilly dilly,
And some to shear corn.
And you and I, dilly dilly,
Will stay so warm.

Lavender's green, dilly dilly,
Lavender's blue.
If you will love me, dilly dilly,
I will love you.
Who told you so, dilly dilly,
Who told you so?
'Twas my own heart, dilly dilly,
That told me so.

Repeat first verse.

Morningtown Ride

The late Malvina Reynolds, was a writer and singer whose diverse repertoire ranged from the feminist to the freewheeling; from the maternal to the environmental. In this fantasy ride to "Morningtown," she invites children on a journey that promises a good night's sleep and sweet dreams.

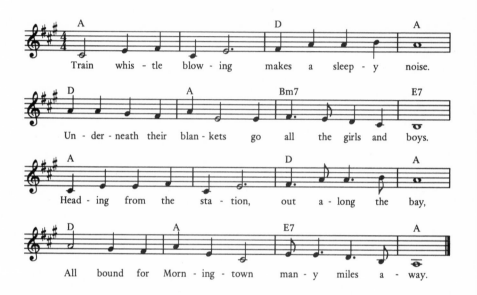

Sarah's at the engine, Tony rings the bell.
John swings the lantern, to show that all is well.
Rocking, rolling, riding, out along the bay,
All bound for Morningtown, many miles away.

Maybe it is raining where our train will ride.
But all the little travellers are snug and warm inside.
Somewhere there is sunshine, somewhere there is day.
Somewhere there is Morningtown, many miles away.

Fais Do-Do

A well-known lullaby, traditional throughout the French-speaking world, its roots are as diverse as the many people who have sung it. From the plantations of Louisiana where it was sung by Creole people in Patois, a combination of French and African languages, to the French-Canadian peoples of Quebec province, this song in its many variations has soothed many a fretful baby to sleep with its beautiful words and calming melody. Your audience will quickly pick up some of the French words if you repeat that version after singing it in English.

Translation:

> Go to sleep, Colas, my little brother,
> Go to sleep and you'll have some cake.
> Mama is upstairs making cakes.
> Papa is downstairs making chocolate.
> Go to sleep, Colas, my little brother,
> Go to sleep and you'll have some cake.

Raindrops

A Slovak lullaby, its mixture of major and minor keys give this a plaintive call as the falling notes echo the "skies weeping" that lull baby to sleep.

By'm Bye

This last lullaby is as familiar as the first in the group, as it appears in countless collections. It is a song to count stars—or children, or fingers, or anything else. It can be used to send a child off to sleep or to send a group off towards home. The first phrases "By'm bye" can be echoed by the group each time you sing it. Its uses are countless as the stars and it will leave everyone shining.

Stars shining,
Number, number four, number five,
Number six.
Good Lord, by'm bye, by'm bye.
Good Lord, by'm bye.

PART V

Resources

Subject Index of Preschool Books

Subject Headings

Subject Index—Preschoolers' Books

Animals

Carle, Eric.	*The Very Quiet Cricket*
Ets, Marie Hall.	*Play With Me*
Flack, Marjorie.	*Ask Mr. Bear*
Fowler, Richard.	*Mr. Little's Noisy Car*
Hutchins, Pat.	*Good Night, Owl*
Kaman, Gloria.	*Paddle, Said the Swan*
Maris, Ron.	*In My Garden*
Martin, Bill.	*Brown Bear, Brown Bear*
Polushkin, Maria.	*Morning*
Rice, Eve.	*Sam Who Never Forgets*
Rogers, Paul.	*What Will the Weather Be Like Today*
Williams, Sue.	*I Went Walking*

Babies

Asch, Frank.	*Baby in the Box*
Carlson, Nancy.	*Poor Carl*
Jonas, Ann.	*When You Were A Baby*

Bears

Asch, Frank.	*Just Like Daddy*
Butler, Dorothy.	*My Brown Bear Barney*
Carlstrom, Nancy.	*Jesse Bear, What Will You Wear*
	Better Not Get Wet, Jesse Bear
Flack, Marjorie.	*Ask Mr. Bear*
Hayes, Sarah.	*This is the Bear and the Picnic Lunch*
Maris, Ron.	*Are You There, Bear*
Watanabe, Shigeo.	*How Do I Put It On?*

Birthdays

Flack, Marjorie.	*Ask Mr. Bear*
Hutchins, Pat.	*Happy Birthday, Sam*

Cars

Fowler, Richard.   *Mr. Little's Noisy Car*
Maestro, Betsy.   *Traffic*

Clothing

Carlstrom, Nancy.   *Jesse Bear, What Will You Wear*
Hutchins, Pat.   *You'll Soon Grow Into Them, Titch*
Rice, Eve.   *Peter's Pockets*
Watanabe, Shigeo.   *How Do I Put It On?*

Colors

Fleming, Denise.   *Lunch*
Kalan, Robert.   *Rain*
Martin, Bill.   *Brown Bear, Brown Bear*
McMillan, Bruck.   *Growing Colors*
Serfozo, Mary.   *Who Said Red?*
Williams, Sue.   *I Went Walking*

Families

Asch, Frank.   *Just Like Daddy*
Carlson, Nancy L.   *Poor Carl*
                                Better Not Get Wet, Jesse Bear
Hutchins, Pat.   *Titch*
                                You'll Soon Grow Into Them, Titch
Kraus, Pat.   *The Carrot Seed*
Rice, Eve.   *Peter's Pockets*

Farm Animals

Brown, Margaret Wise.   *The Big Red Barn*
Galdone, Paul.   *The Little Red Hen*
Maris, Ron.   *Is Anyone Home?*
Stoeke, Janet.   *Minerva Louise*
Waddell, Ron.   *Farmer Duck*

Food

Carle, Eric.	*The Very Hungry Caterpillar*
Fleming, Denise.	*Lunch*
Galdone, Paul.	*The Little Red Hen*
Hayes, Sarah.	*This is the Bear and the Picnic Lunch*
McMillan, Bruce.	*Growing Colors*

Friendship

Carlson, Nancy L.	*I Like Me*
Ets, Marie Hall.	*Play With Me*
Waddell, Martin.	*Farmer Duck*

Gardens

Kraus, Ruth.	*The Carrot Seed*
McMillan, Bruce.	*Growing Colors*

Imagination

Barton, Byron.	*I Want to Be An Astronaut*
Oxenbury, Helen.	*Pippo Gets Lost (Series)*

Imitation

Slobodkina, Esphyr.	*Caps for Sale.*

Jobs

Barton, Byron.	*I Want to Be An Astronaut*
Hill, Eric.	*Who Does What*

Laziness

Galdone, Paul.   *The Little Red Hen*
Waddell, Martin.   *Farmer Duck*

Lift The Flap Books

Fowler, Richard.   *Mr. Little's Noisy Car*
Hill, Eric.   *Who Does What*
Jonas, Ann.   *Where Can It Be?*

Lost Possessions

Galdone, Paul.   *The Three Little Kittens*
Jonas, Ann.   *Where Can It Be?*
Maris, Ron.   *Are You There, Bear?*

Monkeys

Christelow, Eileen.   *Five Little Monkeys*
Slobodkina, Esphyr.   *Caps for Sale*

Numbers

Carle, Eric.   *The Very Hungry Caterpillar*
Christelow, Eileen.   *Five Little Monkeys*
Maris, Ron.   *In My Garden*

Nursery Rhymes

Brown, Ruth.   *Ladybug, Ladybug*
Galdone, Paul.   *The Three Little Kittens*
Hale, Sarah.   *Mary Had a Little Lamb*

Participation Stories

Christelow, Eileen.	*Five Little Monkeys*
Fleming, Denise.	*Lunch*
Hill, Eric.	*Who Does What?*
Martin, Bill.	*Brown Bear, Brown Bear*
Serfozo, Mary.	*Who Said Red?*
Slobodkina, Esphyr.	*Caps for Sale*

Self

Carlson, Nancy L.	*I Like Me*
Martin, Bill.	*Here Are My Hands*

Sleep

Hutchins, Pat.	*Good Night, Owl.*
Kaman, Gloria.	*Paddle Said the Swan.*

Toys

Asch, Frank.	*Baby in the Box*
Jonas, Ann.	*Now We Can Go*
Maris, Ron.	*Are You There, Bear?*
Oxenbury, Helen.	*Pippo Gets Lost (Series)*

Trying

Carle, Eric.	*The Very Quiet Cricket*
Galdone, Paul.	*The Little Red Hen*
Hutchins, Pat.	*Titch*
Kraus, Ruth.	*The Carrot Seed*
Watanabe, Shigeo.	*How Do I Put It On?*

Weather

Deming, Alhambra.	*Who Is Tapping At My Window?*
Kalan, Robert.	*Rain*
Rogers, Paul.	*What Will the Weather Be Like Today?*

Picture Books for Preschool Programs

Asch, Frank. *Baby in the Box*. New York: Holiday House, 1989.

Subject(s): babies, toys

Bright, easy-to-see illustrations and simple, silly text combine to make this a quick, fun read-aloud. Since it is so short, it will work best in combination with other, longer, books.

————. *Just Like Daddy*. New York: Prentice-Hall, 1984.

Subject(s): families, bears

Asch's wry humor is evident in his brief text and expressive illustrations as the little bear tries to do everything "just like Daddy"—even the things Mommy can do best!

Barton, Byron. *I Want to Be an Astronaut*. New York: Crowell, 1988.

Subject(s): imagination, jobs

Barton's simplistic text and illustrations take little ones on a space shuttle, so they can imagine what it would be like if they were astronauts. A great flight.

Brown, Margaret Wise. *Big Red Barn*. Newly illustrated by Felicia Bond. New York: Harper & Row, 1989.

Subject(s): farm animals

Brown's rhymed text introduces the different animals who live at the farm. This new edition, with its larger size and bright illustrations, is just right for storytime.

Brown, Ruth. *Ladybug, Ladybug*. New York: Dutton, 1988.

Subject(s): nursery rhymes

A lovely old-fashioned adaptation of the classic rhyme, with oil-painting illustrations and repeating phrase, "Ladybug, Ladybug," that takes her through the meadow, over the water, the wheat field, and back home again.

Butler, Dorothy. *My Brown Bear Barney*. Illustrated by Elizabeth A. Fuller. New York: Greenwillow Books, 1989.

Subject(s): bears
A little girl and her favorite teddy bear who goes with her everywhere, even, she hopes, school. Butler's repetitive phrase, "My brown bear, Barney" will get little ones involved and Fuller's illustrations add to the enjoyment.

Carle, Eric. *The Very Hungry Caterpillar.* New York: Collins Publishers, 1979.

Subject(s): food, numbers
A classic. The little caterpillar who eats and eats, wraps himself up in his cocoon and becomes a beautiful butterfly. Carle combines text, illustration and book design, using holes and various sized pages, to make this a delightful and interactive experience.

_____. *The Very Quiet Cricket.* New York: Philomel Books, 1990.

Subject(s): animals, trying
A further step in book design for Carle. A young cricket tries to greet other animals by rubbing his wings together but "not a sound" until the very last page when young readers actually "hear" the cricket's success.

Carlson, Nancy L. *I Like Me.* New York: Viking Kestrel, 1988.

Subject(s): friendship, self
By showing off her fine points, "I brush my teeth," "I like my curly tail," a charming young pig decides that she is her own best friend. Big, bordered pictures and one phrase per page help make this one a winner for sharing.

_____. *Poor Carl.* New York: Viking Kestrel, 1989.

Subject(s): babies, families
A subject near and dear to many preschoolers: new babies. This new baby, Carl, is not as lucky as his big brother who can feed himself (and it's not yucky rice cereal), dress himself or play outside with friends. Good thing he has a big brother! Carlson's charming illustrations add to the humor of the text.

Carlstrom, Nancy White. *Jesse Bear, What Will You Wear?* Illustrated by Bruce Degen. New York: Macmillan, 1986.

Subject(s): bears, clothing
With its rhymed text and repeating question in the title, this book fairly sings out a story of its own. Filled with humorous lines, "I'll wear my chair/'Cause I'm stuck there" and brightly colored, bordered illustrations, a book all preschoolers will love.

_____. *Better Not Get Wet, Jesse Bear.* Illustrated by Bruce Degen. New York: Macmillan, 1988.

Subjects: bears, families

Poor Jesse Bear wants to splash with the frog and get a drink with the roses, but it's not until his own wading pool appears that it's okay for Jesse Bear to get wet! A cooling delight for preschoolers who will help you say, "Better not get wet, Jesse Bear!"

Christelow, Eileen, reteller & illus. *Five Little Monkeys Jumping on the Bed.* New York: Clarion Books, 1989.

Subject(s): Monkeys, numbers, participation story

A picture book version of the finger game with illustrations by Christelow filled with charm and humor. Give you preschoolers half a chance and they'll be chiming right in with "No more monkeys jumping on the bed!"

Deming, Alhambra G. *Who is Tapping at My Window?* Illustrated by Monica Wellington. New York: Dutton, 1988.

Subject(s): animals, weather

A little girl asks "Who is tapping at my window?" and one by one different animals respond, "It's not I," until the rain answers "It is I." The bright, flat, bordered pictures and rhyming text give the book its child appeal.

Ets, Marie Hall. *Play with Me.* New York: Viking Press, 1955.

Subject(s): animals, friendship

The classic story of a young girl whose attempts to make friends with the animals around her proves futile—until her quiet sadness brings them all back. Illustrated with pictures containing muted tones of yellows and tans, a simple tale with a satisfying ending.

Flack, Marjorie. *Ask Mr. Bear.* New York: The Macmillan Company, 1932, 1958.

Subject(s): bears, birthdays, animals

A classic picture book. A young boy asks all the animals about a birthday gift for his mother. But nobody has the right answer but Mr. Bear. Old fashioned illustrations lend to its classic, timeless appeal.

Fleming, Denise. *Lunch.* New York: Holt & Co., 1993.

Subject(s): food, colors, participation story

A hungry mouse eats a silly succession of colorful foods. The text and bright, collage-like illustrations give youngsters hints to the foods that appear on the following pages.

Fowler, Richard. *Mr. Little's Noisy Car.* New York: Grosset & Dunlap, 1985.
Subject(s): cars, lift-the-flap story, animals
With large print, stiff pages featuring lift-up flaps, a lively tale of Mr. Little and the menagerie he finds in unlikely places throughout his car.

Galdone, Paul. *Three Little Kittens.* New York: Clarion Books, 1986.
Subject(s): nursery rhymes
With its oversize print and colorful illustrations, a lively and colorful interpretation of the familiar nursery story to which preschoolers will love listening and chanting along.

————. *The Little Red Hen.* New York: Clarion, 1979.
Subject(s): laziness, trying, farm animals, food
The classic tale of the hardworking hen and her lazy friends who are only willing to share the fruits of the hen's hard labors. A story that invites participation.

Hale, Sarah Josepha. *Mary Had a Little Lamb.* Photo-illustrated by Bruce McMillan. New York: Scholastic, 1990.
Subject(s): nursery rhymes
A fresh, contemporary interpretation of the classic tale of young Mary, here portrayed as a black, bespectacled girl, who brings her lamb to school.

Hayes, Sarah. *This is the Bear and the Picnic Lunch.* Illustrated by Helen Craig. Boston: Little, Brown Co., 1988.
Subject(s): bears, food
With a lively rhyming text and illustrations that will appeal to preschoolers, a fun and fanciful tale of a boy, his dog, his bear and their lunch.

Hill, Eric. *Who Does What? Peek-a-Book.* Los Angeles: Price/Stern/Sloan, 1982.
Subject(s): jobs, lift-the-flap books, participation story
In a lively book that invites young listeners' answers, questions are asked about different occupations they will recognize, like mail carriers, mothers, teachers.

Hutchins, Pat. *Good-night, Owl!* New York: Macmillan, 1972.
Subject(s): sleep, animals
With large text and recognizable Hutchins illustrations, a charming cumulative tale of Owl's attempt to sleep while all the other animals keep him awake—until he gets his revenge at night.

_____. *Titch*. New York: Macmillan, 1971.

Subject(s): families, trying

A subject many children understand: being the smallest. With simple sentences telling the tale, Titch must always have the smallest of everything, even the seed that grows into a big plant.

_____. *You'll Soon Grow into Them Titch*. New York: Greenwillow Books, 1983.

Subject(s): families, clothing

Titch is back—and still the smallest. But when even the hand-me-down clothes are too big, he gets nice new clothes, just in time for the nice new baby. Hutchins' clear illustrations, with generous use of white space, are effective in group settings.

_____. *Happy Birthday, Sam*. New York: Greenwillow Books, 1978.

Subject(s): birthdays

This time it's Sam who must cope with being too small for so many things, until his birthday gift from Grandma brings a surprise solution. Hutchins' big illustrations again help to tell the story.

Jonas, Ann. *Now We Can Go*. New York: Greenwillow Books, 1986.

Subject(s): toys

A young child insists on putting all her favorite toys into a big red bag before she is ready to go out with her mom. Jonas uses simple phrasing and boldly colored, graphic illustrations to effectively draw children into the book.

_____. *When You Were a Baby*. New York: Puffin Books, 1986, Greenwillow Books, 1991.

Subject(s): babies

With a simple directness, Jonas talks with young listeners about one of their favorite subjects: how big they are. She does it by reminding them that of all the things they couldn't do as babies that they can do now.

_____. *Where Can It Be?* New York: Greenwillow Books, 1986.

Subject(s): lift-the-flap books, lost possessions

Listeners search throughout the house with the boy in the book for the thing that he's lost and discover that it's his blanket when he finds it at the end of the story.

Kalan, Robert. *Rain*. Illustrated by Donald Crews. New York: Greenwillow Books, 1978 and Mulberry Books, 1991.

Subject(s): colors, weather
Clever combination of color, text and graphics describe a rainfall as it falls on black road, purple flowers, white house and ends in a rainbow.

Kaman, Gloria. *Paddle, Said the Swan.* New York: Atheneum, 1989.

Subject(s): sleep, animals
A soft, quiet rhyming story that listens to each animal mother as they speak to their young. It ends with a baby to whom the mother says "Sleep" and "baby did." Warm, dark-hued watercolors add to the nighttime mood.

Krauss, Ruth. *The Carrot Seed.* Illustrated by Crockett Johnson. New York: Harper, 1945, Harper & Row, 1989, Harper Festival, 1993.

Subject(s); gardens, trying, families
A classic small book with a big message: try and you'll succeed. With few words and charming yellow and brown-toned illustrations, a book that will succeed on many levels.

Maestro, Betsy and Guilio Maestro. *Traffic: A Book of Opposites.* New York: Crown, 1981.

Subject(s): cars
Large words on each page accompany a little car on its journey through a brightly illustrated landscape to demonstrate words like fast, slow, stop and go.

Maris, Ron. *Are You There, Bear?* New York: Greenwillow Books, 1984.

Subject(s): bears, toys, lost possessions
Preschoolers will love going on this hunt for bear. With an effective use of light and dark, a light is used to search a dark room, ask of various other toys, "Are you there, bear?"

————. *In My Garden.* New York: Greenwillow Books, 1987.

Subject(s): animals, numbers
Rhyming phrases describe and alternating half-pages reveal everything a girl finds in her outdoor explorations. Animals, numbers and hidden objects combine here to charm preschoolers.

————. *Is Anyone Home?* New York: Greenwillow Books, 1985.

Subject(s): farm animals
Using the same technique of simple text and half-pages, a young child greets all the animals on her grandparents' farm.

Martin, Bill, Jr. *Brown Bear, Brown Bear, What Do You See?* Illustrated by Eric Carle. New York: Holt, Rinehart and Winston, 1983, Holt & Co., 1992.

Subject(s): colors, animals, participation story

One of the classic color books. As each animal is introduced, he is asked "What do you see?" and he then introduces the next, from a yellow duck to a purple cat. It invites interaction. A sure winner.

————, and John Archambault. *Here Are My Hands.* Illustrated by Ted Rand. New York: Holt & Co., 1987, 1989.

Subject(s): self

Twelve children of all shapes, sizes and colors point out all the parts of them and their uses. There are "hands . . . for catching and throwing" and "cheeks for kissing and blushing." Its rhyming text and pastel illustrations make this a favorite among the preschool crowd.

McMillan, Bruce. *Growing Colors.* New York: Lothrop, Lee & Shepard Books, 1988.

Subject(s): colors, gardens, food

Photographs of different colored fruits and vegetables give young listeners a chance to see—and guess at—many familiar and not-so-familiar foods.

Oxenbury, Helen. *Pippo Gets Lost.* New York: Aladdin Books, 1989.

Subject(s): toys, imagination

One of a series with Tom and his stuffed friend, Pippo. Its slightly stiff pages and alternating fine line drawings and full color illustrations give this charming series a child's view of many of life's little problems.

Polushkin, Maria. *Morning.* Illustrated by Bill Morrison. New York: Four Winds Press, 1983.

Subject(s): animals

With minimalist text, three-color illustrations and wry humor, the story of a farm morning. One by one, the animals wake up, and a boy goes out to catch a fish to fry for breakfast—making a mess in the process.

Rice, Eve. *Peter's Pockets.* Illustrated by Nancy Winslow. Parker, New York: Greenwillow Books, 1989.

Subject(s); clothing, family

Peter goes for a walk with his uncle Nick and discovers he has no pockets to hold all the treasures he finds. But Mom has an ingenious solution when they return. Parker's childlike illustrations add their own appeal to the story.

_____. *Sam Who Never Forgets*. Illustrated by Kazuko. New York: Greenwillow Books, 1977.

Subject(s): zoo animals
A favorite with the preschool set, the tale of faithful Sam, who would never forget to feed the elephant! Its simple story and Kazuko's quiet illustrations are a perfect combination.

Rogers, Paul. *What Will the Weather Be Like Today?* Illustrated by Kazuko. New York: Greenwillow Books, 1990.

Subject(s): weather, animals
A story about all kinds of weather and the different animals that enjoy each kind. Kazuko's flat, patchwork-like illustrations are the perfect accompaniment.

Serfozo, Mary. *Who Said Red?* Illustrated by Keiko Narahashi. New York: Margaret K. McElderry Books, 1988, Aladdin Books, 1992.

Subject(s): colors, participation story
Splashy watercolors and lyrical text make this a charming combination of color story and interactive book. By the end, to answer the question, everyone will join in with the answer: "I said red!"

Slobodkina, Esphyr. *Caps For Sale; A Tale of a Pedlar, Some Monkeys, and Their Monkey Business*. New York: W. R. Scott, 1947. Harper & Row, 1987.

Subject(s): monkeys, imitation, participation story
The classic story of the pedlar who couldn't sell his caps but who got mixed up in monkey business after a noontime nap. A longer story which can work with preschoolers because of its opportunity for repetition and participation.

Stoeke, Janet Morgan. *Minerva Louise*. New York: E. P. Dutton, 1988.

Subject(s): farm animals
Told with the right humor for three-year-olds, the story of the poor little hen Minerva Louise, who tries to make a house meant for humans just right for her.

Waddell, Martin. *Farmer Duck*. Illustrated by Helen Oxenbury. Cambridge: Candlewick Press, 1992.

Subject(s): farm animals, laziness, friendship
The tale of a duck whose life of work for a lazy farmer finally forces him, along with the help of the other animals, to rebel. Oxenbury's expressive watercolor illustrations add warmth and personality to this tale of justice.

Watanabe, Shigeo. *How Do I Put It On?* Illustrated by Yasuo Ohtomo. New York: Philomel Books, 1979.

Subject(s): bears, clothing, participation story

One of a series of whimsical books by Watanabe that explores the small problems and achievements of a young bear's world. Here a young bear asks the reader about the right and wrong ways to put on shirt, shoes, cap and pants, with amusing results.

Williams, Sue. *I Went Walking.* Illustrated by Julie Vivas. San Diego: Harcourt Brace Jovanovich, 1990.

Subject(s): colors, animals

With phrasing reminiscent of *Brown Bear, Brown Bear,* a young girl goes on a walk and sees different colored animals, brown horse, black cat, green duck, pink pig, who all follow her into a riotous final page. Large watercolor illustrations and simple text combine to invite participation.

Songs in Picture-Book Form

Many songs for children have also been published in picture-book form. The titles listed here are only the picture-book renditions of the songs that are included in this book. Five of the songs have two versions included and more than half of the picture books provide the music to the songs. But all are wonderful examples of the way that songs tell a story. As your own repertoire grows, you will discover many other songs that have also been rendered into picture-book form, so keep adding to this list. Only one book included here is also listed with the Picture Books for Preschool Programs. But all of these can also become part of your preschooler program, both as read-alouds or as display books that parents can then borrow.

Chase, Richard, ed. *Billy Boy.* Illustrated by Glen Rounds. San Carlos, Calif: Golden Gate Junior Books, 1966. (O.P.)
(Melody included)
With his riotous illustrations, Glen Rounds transforms this glimpse at pioneer days into a lively story.

Christelow, Eileen, reteller & illus. *Five Little Monkeys Jumping On the Bed.* New York: Clarion Books, 1989.
(No Melody)
An extended version of the rhyme into story makes this book a combination of finger game, counting book and song.

Conover, Chris, reteller & illus. *Six Little Ducks.* New York: Crowell, 1976.
(Melody Included)
A variation on the traditional song. Here, the six little ducks go to market with a quack, quack, quack. Bordered pen & ink illustrations, and some full color two-page spreads give the book an old-fashioned look and feel.

The Fox Went Out On a Chilly Night. Illustrated by Peter Spier. Garden City, N.Y.: Doubleday, 1961.

(Melody included)

With a single line of verse running through two page spreads of alternating pen-and-ink and then full-color illustrations, a Caldecott Honor book that transforms this song into a compelling story.

Garelick, May. *Just My Size.* Illustrated by William Pene Du Bois. New York: Harper & Row, 1990.

(No Melody)

A variation on the theme found in the song "I Had an Old Coat." Here, a little girl tells about her coat and what it became as she outgrew it, but still found uses for it.

Hush Little Baby, A Folk Lullaby. Illustrated by Aliki. Englewood Cliffs, N.J.: Prentice-Hall, 1968.

(Melody included)

With her soft illustrations that resemble paintings done on wood, Aliki renders this classic lullaby into story form.

Hush, Little Baby. Illustrated by Margot Zemach. Harmondsworth: Kestrel Books, 1976.

(Melody included)

The classic lullaby that promises baby all sorts of presents, if he'll only stop crying. Watercolors depict a "large untidy Mum" and "downtrodden Dad" promising baby anything to hush.

I Know an Old Lady Who Swallowed a Fly. Illustrated by Glen Rounds. New York: Holiday House, 1990.

(No Melody)

Who doesn't know that old lady who kept swallowing animals? Well, here's a lively illustrated version with an old lady, a fly and assorted other critters like no other. Even the different sized text tells the story.

Kovalski, Maryann, reteller & illus. *The Wheels On the Bus.* Boston: Joy Street Books, 1987.

(Melody included)

A colorful, lively story in which a grandmother and grandchildren enjoy singing the song so much as they wait at the bus stop, that they miss the bus and have to take a taxi!

Langstaff, John, reteller. *Frog Went A'Courtin*. Illustrated by Feodor Rojankovsky. New York: Harcourt, Brace, 1955.

(Melody included)

An illustrated version of the well-known American folksong about the amorous frog and his true love.

————, reteller. *Over In the Meadow*. Illustrated by Feodor Rojankovsky. New York: Harcourt, Brace, 1975. Music by Marshall Woodbridge.

(Melody Included)

An illustrated version of the traditional song, adapted by Langstaff, with pictures as gentle as the words.

Over in the Meadow. Illustrated by Ezra Jack Keats New York: Four Winds Press, 1971.

(No Melody)

The animal counting game, illustrated in Keats' rich watercolors.

Raffi. *Down By The Bay*. Illustrated by Nadine Bernard Westcost. "A Raffi Song To Read". New York: Crown Publishers, 1987.

(Melody included)

A picture book version of Raffi's rendition of the traditional song, with wild illustrations that make the silly verses even sillier.

————. *Shake My Sillies Out*. Illustrated by David Allender. "A Raffi Song to Read". New York: Crown Publishers, 1987.

(Melody included)

A picture book that turns the popular song about shaking, jumping and yawning into a story about animals, campers, disconcerted adults, and just plain silliness.

Rounds, Glen, reteller & illus. *Sweet Betsy From Pike*. Chicago: Children's Press, 1973. (O.P.)

(No Melody)

The saga of Betsy and Ike as they traveled west to seek their fortunes, with certain verses selected and illustrated in pen & ink by Rounds.

Staines, Bill. *All God's Critters Got a Place in the Choir*. Illustrated by Margot Zemach. New York: E. P. Dutton, 1989.

(Melody included)

A tale of animals, some who sing high, some who sing low and some who just clap their hands or paws.

Wendy Watson's Frog Went A-Courting. New York: Lothrop, Lee & Shepard Books, 1990.

(Melody included)

Another version of the lovesick frog and his courting adventures, told with full verses beneath bordered softly shaded illustrations that come in all sizes until, at the end, the figures are jumping all over the final page.

Westcott, Nadine Bernard, retel. & illus. *Skip to My Lou.* Boston: Joy Street Books, 1989.

(Melody included)

The classic American folksong that in this form uses many of the livelier verses such as, "Pigs in the parlor, what'll I do?" to turn the song into an amusing and freewheeling tale of a big mess cleaned up in the nick of time.

Zelinsky, Paul, adapt. & illus. *The Wheels on the Bus.* Paper engineering by Roger Smith. New York: Dutton's Children's Books, 1990.

(Melody included)

With lively pictures and durable paper engineering, here's a version of the favorite song with wheels that go round and round and windows that go up and down as the bus goes all through the town.

Story Suggestions

Here are suggestions for stories covering a variety of styles and moods. Long, short, silly, or sad, they are tellable, enjoyable stories that you can share with audiences over and over. Sources and a brief description of the story, accompany each suggestion. Many of these stories derive from picture books. But, except for those that were written by a specific author, almost every story suggested here can be located in a number of different sources and in several different versions. So, if you like a particular story but the version in the source suggested here is not your style, please seek others that might work better for you.

Anansi and The Moss Covered Rock, an Anansi tale retold in a picture book by Eric Kimmel and illustrated by Janet Stevens (Holiday House, 1988).

A trickster tale in which the wily Anansi uses a magic rock to steal each animal's food but is finally outwitted by small, shy, bush deer. There are opportunities for audience participation each time the magic rock works its spell. This can also be told in tandem with one teller taking the part of Anansi and the other taking the part of each animal as he gets tricked. The humor builds with the anticipation until the wonderful climax, when Anansi gets his due.

The Banza, a tale from Haiti adapted to picture-book form by Diane Wolkstein and illustrated by Marc Tolen Brown (Dial Press, 1981).

It is a story of true friendship between a goat and a tiger, as the tiger's gift of a banza, or little banjo, to Cabree, the goat, shows the goat how her heart—and her song—can protect her. Audiences can join in with Cabree as she sings her song.

The Camel Who Took a Walk, an original story told in a picture book by Jack Tworkov and illustrated by Roger Duvoisin (Aladdin Books, 1951).

A cumulative tale about a camel, a tiger, a monkey, and several other assorted animals in the forest, this story builds anticipation to a climax that is a bit different from what you would expect!

"Coyote Helps Decorate the Night," retold by Harold Courlander in his collection, *People of the Short Blue Corn: Tales and Legends of the Hopi Indians* (Harcourt Brace Jovanovitch, 1970).

A trickster tale in which Coyote is too lazy to help decorate the earth—until his curiosity gets the best of him! Also available on *Tales in the Wind*, an audiocassette of tales told by Marcia Lane (Gentle Wind, 1984) and in *From Sea to Shining Sea*, compiled by Amy Cohen (Scholastic, 1993).

The Dancing Skeleton, by Cynthia DeFelice with illustrations by Robert Andrew Parker (Macmillan, 1989).

A lively tale for Halloween about Aaron Kelly who was (almost) dead, his poor widow, and the fiddler who courted her and fiddled Aaron back into his grave. This has lots of energy and cracking bones.

Elephant in a Well, by Marie Hall Ets. (Viking Press, 1972).

A cumulative story in the same spirit as "The Enormous Turnip," as a succession of animals join in to help pull out poor Elephant, who got stuck in the well because he didn't watch where he was going.

The Enormous Turnip, from a classic Russian tale, adapted and illustrated by Kathy Parkinson in a picture-book version (Albert Whitman, 1986).

A rollicking cumulative tale in which each family member joins in to try and pull the enormous turnip out of the ground. Many retellings of this story are available in collections, as well. Opportunities for participation and creative dramatics, as well as flannel board possibilities, make this story a fun and versatile choice.

Georgie, written and illustrated by Robert Bright (Doubleday, Doran, and Co., 1944).

A classic original story that is a popular picture book, this also makes a good story to tell. It is appealing to younger audiences, as Georgie the ghost finds himself without a house to haunt. Ghostly sounds present possibilities for audience participation.

Greyling: A Picture Story from the Islands of Shetland, an original story, written by Jane Yolen and originally illustrated by William Stobbs (World Publishing Co., 1968), a second edition of this picture book has been newly illustrated by David Ray (Philomel, 1991).

The haunting story of the fisherman and his wife, who long for a child and find a selchie they raise and love and eventually must give up. A traditional folk song from the Scottish islands of Shetland and Orkney, "The Great Selchie of Sule Skerrie," is included at the end of the book.

The Hobyahs, retold and illustrated as a picture book by Simon Stern (Prentice Hall, 1977).

A favorite at Halloween, this tale is found in several versions—from grisly to gentle. Stern's telling is appropriate for groups with a wide age range, as it is a bit more gentle than some others: the little dog, Turpie, remains intact, and only gets put in a box. Audiences can also have the opportunity to join in the "Hobyah, hobyah, hobyah" chant, so they won't be so scared.

"How Buzzard Got His Feathers," from *Iroquois Stories: Heroes and Heroines, Monsters and Magic,* collected by Joseph Bruchac, illustrated by Daniel Burgevin (The Crossing Press, 1985).

An Iroquois story about Buzzard, whose vanity gets the best of him when he is chosen to bring back suits of feathers to clothe the other birds. Although he is given first choice by the Creator, he rejects all the other suits and must be content with an ill-fitting suit of dull, brown feathers.

Lazy Jack, illustrated and retold by Tony Ross (Dial Book for Young Readers, 1986).

A tale steeped in oral tradition, with many versions from many different countries. This version has Tony Ross's own zany twists, but tells the story of poor, witless Jack, who can never figure quite the right way to carry anything home.

Little Red Hen, illustrated and adapted by Paul Galdone (Seabury Press, 1973).

A favorite with younger audiences for its repeating refrain, its possibilities for creative dramatics and flannel-board telling, and its predictable, satisfying ending.

"The Lion and The Rabbit," adapted by Heather Forest and found in *Joining In, An Anthology of Audience Participation Stories and How to Tell Them,* compiled by Teresa Miller (Yellow Moon Press, 1988).

This ancient fable from India uses the element of "echo" to invite audience participation in the plot about an old, wise rabbit who outwits a strong, but stupid, lion.

Millions of Cats. An original, now classic, tale by Wanda Gág, (Coward-McCann, 1928).

This tells of the little old man and woman who couldn't decide which cat to keep of the hundreds, millions, billions, and trillions of cats. The repetitious refrain is tailor-made for participation, making this a favorite with younger audiences.

The Princess and The Pea, by Hans Christian Andersen. (North-South Books, 1985).

One of the shortest and best known of Andersen's tales is illustrated in this picture-book version by Dorothee Duntze. A princess must prove her princess potential by showing her sensitivity to a pea—hundreds of mattresses below.

"Sody Sallyratus," available in many different collections, including *Twenty Tellable Tales,* by Margaret Read MacDonald (H. W. Wilson, 1986).

An Appalachian tale about an old woman, an old man, a boy, a girl, a squirrel, baking soda and a bear! The repetition and silliness of the tale cry out for audiences to join in with each character as they skip their way down the hill, singing about buying, "Sody, sody, sody sallyratus!"

The Three Billy Goats Gruff, adapted and illustrated by Paul Galdone (Seabury Press, 1973).

This tale from Denmark has become a classic picture book, but is still a great story to tell. Children of all ages will enjoy "trip, trapping" over the bridge with each goat and roaring like the troll who is finally done for.

The Three Sillies, Adapted and illustrated by Paul Galdone (Clarion Books, 1981) from an English folktale first collected by Joseph Jacobs.

A young man goes off to find three bigger sillies than his own dear silly and her parents before he will marry her. Chock full of silliness that is sure to bring plenty of giggles.

Tikki, Tikki, Tembo, an ancient tale of China retold by Arlene Mosel and illustrated by Blair Lent (Holt & Co., 1968).

A well-known, often-told tale of the two sons, the younger one with the short, plain name and the older one with the longer, more complicated name who almost drowns in the well because of it. His long, difficult, oft-chanted name is a great spur to audience participation.

"The Tinker and the Ghost," available in *When the Lights Go Out* by Margaret Read MacDonald (H. W. Wilson, 1988) and in a picture-book version, *The Boy and the Ghost,* written by Robert San Souci and illustrated by Jerry Pinkney (Simon & Schuster, 1992).

An old tale for Halloween with bones flying and a stalwart hero who refuses to be afraid, this has lots of repeated phrases and action that make it great fun for interactive listening.

The Vanishing Pumpkin, an original story in picture-book form written by Tony Johntson, illustrated by Tomie De Paola (Putnam, 1983).

Join with the seven-hundred-year-old woman and the eight-hundred-year-old man as they search for their missing pumpkin. The variety of characters and the opportunities for your audience to join in making this a rollicking choice for Halloween.

We're Going on a Bear Hunt, Long a traditional chant/story, this has recently been adapted as a picture book by Michael Rosen, with illustrations by Helen Oxenbury (Margaret K. McElderry Books, 1989).

With the book or as a chant, this story can lead you and your group into a hunt for a bear that will yield nothing but fun.

What Do You Do with a Kangaroo?, an original story in a picture book written and illustrated by Mercer Mayer (Four Winds Press, 1974).

This story can be told in tandem, with each of two tellers asking in turn, "What do you do?" about each of the animals that could suddenly appear in your house. Or, it can work just as well with a single storyteller. The question this story asks leads, inevitably, to audience response—and great hilarity.

Storytelling Resources

This list is a sampling of the many storytelling source books that can help with technique, theory and the telling of tales. There are also countless collections of stories, from all different cultures and countries, from which to choose, as well as many classic tellable stories that have been reprinted in picture-book form.

Baker, Augusta, and Ellin Greene. *Storytelling Art and Technique.* New York: R. R. Bowker, 1977.

>One of the basic tools for beginning storytellers. Filled with practical, comforting advice and tips on every aspect of storytelling.

Bauer, Carolyn Feller. *Handbook for Storytellers.* Chicago: American Library Association, 1977, 1992.

>A comprehensive resource that discusses such things as putting a storytelling program together, narrative and non-narrative sources of folklore, puppetry, storyboards, magic and music. Many bibliographies included.

Clarkson, Atelia, and Gilbert B. Cross, ed. *World Folktales.* New York: Scribner, 1980.

>A wide-ranging collection of stories divided by category of tales, with notes on telling and on different versions included.

Cohn, Amy. *From Sea to Shining Sea: A Treasury of American Folklore and Folk Songs.* Illustrated by eleven Caldecott winners. New York: Scholastic, 1993.

>A true treasure trove with folk stories, songs, and poetry that celebrates America's past and present.

Goode, Diane, comp & illus. *The Diane Goode Book of American Folk Tales and Songs.* New York: Dutton, 1989.

>An attractive compilation of both familiar and obscure tales and songs.

Livo, Norma J., and Sandra A. Rietz. *Storytelling, Process and Practice.* Colorado: Libraries Unlimited, 1986.

A scholarly approach and discussion of storytelling as well as practical ideas and resources.

MacDonald, Margaret R. *Look Back and See. Twenty Lively Tales for Gentle Tellers*. illustrations by Roxanne Murphy. Bronx, N.Y.: H. W. Wilson, 1991.

A collection of tales from many cultures that promote a non-violent world view. With notes on telling and sources.

_____. *The Storyteller's Sourcebook. A Subject, Title, and Motif Index to Folklore Collections for Children*. Neal-Schuman Publishers, Inc., 1982.

A wide-ranging list of subjects and motifs culled from tales in over 900 sources. A valuable resource for storytellers on all levels.

_____. *Twenty Tellable Tales. Audience Participation Folktales for the Beginning Storyteller*. Bronx, N.Y.: H. W. Wilson, 1986.

Stories presented in "ethnopoetic" form, with notes on telling and sources, a valuable source for the beginning storyteller.

_____. *When The Lights Go Out. Scary Tales to Tell*. Bronx, N.Y.: H. W. Wilson, 1988.

A collection of twenty stories that range from the not-too-scary to the really gross stuff.

Miller, Teresa, comp. *Joining In. An Anthology of Audience Participation Stories and How to Tell Them*. Cambridge, Mass: Yellow Moon Press, 1988.

A collection of eighteen stories of varying lengths and themes, complete with notes on telling and audience response.

Pellowski, Anne. *The Family Storytelling Handbook: How to Use Stories, Anecdotes, Rhymes, Handkerchiefs, Paper, and Other Objects to Enrich Your Family Traditions*. New York: Macmillan, 1987.

An exploration of ways to bring storytelling alive in your home.

_____. *Hidden Stories in Plants: Unusual and Easy-to-Tell Stories From Around the World, Together with Creative Things to Do While Telling Them*. New York: Macmillan, 1990.

An unusual way to bring nature into your storytelling experience.

_____. *The Story Vine: A Source Book of Unusual and Easy-to-Tell Stories from Around the World*. Illustrated by Lynn Sweat. New York: Macmillan, 1984.

Ways to tell stories with string.

_____. *The World of Storytelling.* Expanded and Rev. ed. Bronx, N.Y.: H. W. Wilson, 1990.

A scholarly and comprehensive study of the history and tradition of storytelling as well as the many forms stories can take.

Schimmel, Nancy. *Just Enough to Make a Story: A Sourcebook for Storytelling.* Berkeley: Sisters Choice Press, 1978, 1992.

A small collection of stories, as well as discussion of the art and technique of storytelling.

Sierra, Judy. *The Flannel Board Storytelling Book.* Bronx, N.Y.: H. W. Wilson, 1987.

Thirty-six short stories, poems, and songs for use in flannel board storytelling to children ages three to twelve. Easy-to-copy patterns for figures as well as guides to telling are included.

_____ and Robert Kaminski. *Multicultural Folktales: Stories to Tell Young Children.* Selected translations by Adela Artola Allen. Phoenix, AR: The Oryx Press, 1991.

Stories for children from two-and-one-half to five from a variety of cultures, with patterns and tips on flannel board and puppet use with telling. Storytelling tips and resources included.

_____. *Twice Upon a Time. Stories To Tell, Retell, Act Out and Write About.* Bronx, N.Y.: H. W. Wilson, 1989.

Exploring ways to extend storytelling with writing and creative dramatics. A good source for the classroom.

Tashjian, Virginia A., comp. *Juba This and Juba That: Story Hour Stretches for Large or Small Groups.* Illustrated by Victoria De Larrea. Boston: Little Brown, 1969.

A hodgepodge of stories, rhymes, fingerplays, songs and fun.

_____, comp. *With a Deep Sea Smile: Story Hour Stretches for Large or Small Groups.* Illustrated by Rosemary Wells. Boston: Little, Brown & Co., 1974.

A second collection of chants, poems, finger plays, songs and fun for use in story hours.

Song Collections

Axelrod, Alan, and Dan Fox. *Songs of the Wild West.* Illustrated with art work from The Metropolitan Museum of Art. Published by The Metropolitan Museum of Art in Association with the Buffalo Bill Historical Center. 1992.

An assortment of songs that celebrate the life and land of the cowboy, the settler and the Native American.

Glazer, Tom. *Tom Glazer's Treasury of Songs for Children.* (Revised edition of *Tom Glazer's Treasury of Folk Songs, 1964*) Illustrated by John O'Brien. Garden City, N.Y., 1983.

A feast of singing for children from holiday songs to spirituals to everything in between.

————. *The Mother Goose Songbook.* Illustrated by David M. McPhail. New York: Doubleday, 1990.

Many of Mother Goose's favorites, along with some new lyrics and McPhail's wild and singular illustrations.

————. *Music for Ones and Twos: Songs and Games for the Very Young Child.* Illustrated by Karen Ann Weinhaus. Garden City, N.Y.: Doubleday, 1983.

A lively collection of classic and original songs and finger plays.

Guthrie, Woody. *Woody's 20 Grow Big Songs: Song and Pictures.* Illustrated by Marjorie Guthrie. New York: HarperCollins, 1992.

A long lost music book of Guthrie's songs, recently found and published.

An Illustrated Treasury of Song: The National Gallery of Art. Illustrated with art works from The National Gallery. New York: Rizzoli, 1991.

A handsome collection containing many familiar, classic tunes.

Krull, Kathleen, comp. *Gonna Sing My Head off!: American Folk Songs for Children.* Illustrated by Allen Garns. New York: A. A. Knopf, 1990.

A wide-ranging collection of classic and favorite songs for children of all ages.

Langstaff, John, comp. *Climbing Jacob's Ladder: Heroes of the Bible in African-American Spirituals.* Illustrated by Ashley Bryant. Musical arrangements by John Andrew Ross. New York: Margaret K. McElderry Books, 1991.

A collection of spirituals from the Black American tradition that sing about Old Testament heroes.

Larrick, Nancy, ed. *Songs From Mother Goose: With the Traditional Melody for Each.* New York: Harper & Row, 1989. Illustrated by Robin Spowart.

A collection of some classic rhymes and their melodies.

————. *The Wheels of the Bus Go Round and Round.* Illustrated by Gene Holtan. San Carlos, CA: Golden Gate Junior Books, 1972.

A collection of school bus and schoolyard chants, songs and rhymes, some familiar, some maybe not.

Raffi. *The Raffi Everything Grows Songbook: A Collection of Songs From Raffi's Album Everything Grows.* New York: Crown Publishers, 1989.

The third collection of songs from this popular Canadian singer, with illustrations by children.

Raposo, Joe, and Jeffrey Moss. *The Sesame Street Song Book.* Arrangements by Sy Oliver. Illustrated by Loretta Trezzo. New York: Simon and Schuster in conjunction with Children's Television Workshop, 1971.

Words and music for thirty-six songs from the classic television show.

Sharon, Lois and Bram. *Sharon, Lois and Bram's Mother Goose: Songs, Finger Rhymes, Tickling Verses, Games and More.* Illustrated by Maryann Kovalski. New York: The Atlantic Monthly Press, 1985.

A confection of singing, swaying, and chanting treats from the famous trio.

Warren Mattox, Cheryl. *Shake it to the One That You Love the Best: Play Songs and Lullabies from Black Musical Traditions.* Nashville: JTC of Nashville, 1989.

A collection of songs, games, chants and lullabies steeped in the African-American tradition.

Yolen, Jane, ed. *The Lullaby Songbook.* Musical arrangements by Adam Stemple. Illustrated by Charles Mikolaycak. San Diego: Harcourt, Brace, Jovanovich, 1986.

A small, gentle collection of lullabies from a variety of places.

Songs in Recorded Collections

The tapes listed here cover a wide variety of artists and songs. Although each of the artists on this list has his/her own style, they all share a love for songs and for sharing them with children and adults. Many of these collections have songs that are included in this book. In such cases, the names of those songs have been listed after the annotations of the tape collections. Many of the more popular songs are repeated on a few different tapes. If you have access to different versions, it will give you an opportunity to listen to a variety of singing styles, as well as the songs themselves. If you have some of these tape collections in your library, be sure to display them, as this will give your patrons the opportunity to bring some of the songs home with them.

Bartels, Joanie. *Travelin' Magic.* Sherman Oaks, Calif.: Discovery Music, 1988.

A tape of songs with words and music on one side, just music on the other. *Songs included:* "Wheels on the Bus."

Booker, Cedella Marley. *Smilin' Island of Song: A Musical Adventure for Children.* Redway, Calif.: Music for Little People, 1992.

A musical trip to Jamaica, with songs that bring the tropical island right to you.
Songs included: "Brown Girl in the Ring."

Buchman, Rachel. *Hello Everybody.* Albany, N.Y.: A Gentle Wind, 1986.

A collection of pretend and play songs for toddlers.
Songs included: "Little Red Wagon."

Cafra, Pat. *Babes, Beasts and Birds.* Scarborough, Ont.: A&M Records, 1978.

Songs and lullabies for toddlers.
Songs included: "When the Cows Get Up in the Morning," "Skip to My Lou," "Over in the Meadow," and "By'n Bye."

Glazer, Tom. *Music for Ones and Twos.* Mount Vernon, N.Y.: CMS Records, 1972.

Music for baby and toddler about everyday life, from bathtime to bedtime.

197

Guthrie, Woody. *Songs to Grow On, Vol. 0 for Mother and Child* New York: Folkways Records, 1956.

Gentle songs written and sung by Woody.

Hallum, Rosemary. *Fingerplays and Footplays*. Freeport, New York: Educational Activities, 1987.

A collection of classic children's songs, filled with action.
Songs included: "Two Little Blackbirds," "Five Little Monkeys," "The Wheels on the Bus."

Harley, Bill. *Big, Big World*. Hollywood, CA: A&M Records, Inc. 1993.

A little bit of everything: environment, pretending, friendship, but all of it with Bill Harley's slightly wild outlook.
Songs included: "So Long, My Mom."

Hoffman, Nan, and Friends. *Ahead of the Game*. Swormville, N.Y.: Nan Hoffman, 1985.

A collection of songs by a variety of artists on different subjects.
Songs included: "I'm Gonna Tell," "Going to the Zoo," "Magic Penny," "I Had an Old Coat," "All Gods Critters Have a Place in the Choir."

Jenkins, Ella. *And One and Two and Other Songs for Preschool and Primary Children*. New York: Folkways, 1971.

Songs that explore rhythms, movement and counting for young children.

_____. *Counting Games and Rhythms for the One*. New York: Folkways Records, 1965.

Showing her talent for engaging children in her enjoyment of music, Ella Jenkins shares songs and games with the children on the tape (as well as those who are listening to it).
Songs included: "Two Little Blackbirds."

_____. *Hopping Around from Place to Place*. Voices of The Chicago Children's Choir, pamphlet with lyrics included. Freeport, N.Y.: Activity Records, 1983.

Ella and kids enjoying songs about various places.

_____. *You'll Sing a Song and I'll Sing a Song*. Voices of the Urban Gateways Children's Chorus. New York: Folkways Cassette, 1966.

A collection of classic and original call-and-response songs. Songs included: "You'll Sing a Song and I'll Sing a Song."

Johnson, Laura. *Homemade Games and Activities*. Long Branch, N.J.: Kimbo Educational, 1987.

A gentle collection of familiar and original, singable songs that include games to help children develop listening as well as motor skills.
Songs included: "When Pigs Get Up in the Morning."

McGrath, Bob. *Sing Along with Bob*. Toronto, Ont.: Kids Records, 1985.

Bob singing a collection of very familiar and singable songs.
Songs included: "If You're Happy and You Know It," "The Wheels on the Bus," "Six Little Ducks," "Five Little Monkeys," "Head and Shoulders," "Skip to My Lou," "Mr. Sun," "She'll Be Comin' Round the Mountain."

McGrath, Bob, and Kathrine Smithrine. *Songs and Games for Toddlers*. Scarborough, Ont.: A&M Records of Canada, Ltd., 1985.

A tape developed from Smithrine's classes for two's and three's that dealt with music and movement.
Songs included: "Bumpin' Up and Down."

Monet, Lisa. *Circle Time Sound Recording*. Redway, Ca.: Music for Little People, 1986.

Classic and familiar songs and fingerplays, all arranged by Monet.
Songs included: "If You're Happy," "Itsy Bitsy Spider," "All Through the Town," "Two Little Blackbirds," "Head and Shoulders."

———. *Jump Down: Songs and Games*. Ferndale, Ca.: Circle Sound Productions, 1987.

More of the same idea as *Circle Time*, with familiar and singable songs.
Songs included: "Roll Over," "Bingo."

Musical Munchkins. *Makin' Music*. Pound Ridge, N.Y.: Musical Munchkins, 1989.

Kids, grown-ups, and different instruments combine to enjoy songs.
Songs included: "Two Little Blackbirds," "When Ducks Get Up," "Over in the Meadow."

Raffi. A *Children's Sampler*. Willowdale, Ont.: Troubadour Records, 1986.

Familiar and popular Raffi, with lots of songs kids will recognize.
Songs included: "You'll Sing a Song," "Six Little Ducks," and "Wheels on the Bus."

_____. *Everything Grows*. Willowdale, Ont.: Shoreline/A&M Records, 1987.
A newer crop of songs all about growing.

_____. *More Singable Songs*. Willowdale, Ont.: Troubadour Records, 1977.
Always a hit, Raffi's songs are easy listening and easy singing.
Songs included: "Six Little Ducks," "Sodeo."

_____. *One Light, One Sun*. Willowdale, Ont.: Troubadour Records, 1985.
A crop of singable hits.
Songs included: "Down on Grandpa's Farm," "In My Garden."

_____. *Rise and Shine*. Willowdale, Ont.: Troubadour Records, 1982.
Another in a line-up of sure-fire winners.
Songs included: "Ducks Like Rain."

_____. *Singable Songs for the Very Young*. Willowdale, Ont.: Troubadour Records, 1976.
Lots of classic songs done Raffi's way.
Songs included: "Down by the Bay," "Bumping Up and Down," "Mr. Sun," "To the Zoo."

Seeger, Pete. *Birds, Beasts, Bugs, and Bigger Fishes*. New York: Folkways Records, 1954.
A collection of true, classic folk songs, done by a real American troubadour.
Songs included: "Leatherwing Bat."

_____. *Stories and Songs for Little Children*. Fairview, N.C.: High Windy Audio, 1987.
The quintessential folk singer sharing classic songs with children.
Songs included: "Skip to My Lou," "Frog Went A-Courtin'," "She'll Be Comin' Round the Mountain."

Sharon, Lois & Bram. *Happy Birthday*. Toronto: Elephant Records, 1988.
A party in itself with games, songs, and tons of fun for everyone.
Songs included: "All the Pretty Little Horses."

_____. *One Elephant*. Toronto: Elephant Records, 1978.
One elephant, three singers, and lots of songs that have Sharon, Lois, and Bram's special brand. Perfect for kids.
Songs included: "Five Little Monkeys," "She'll Be Comin' Round the Mountain."

————. *Sing A to Z*. Toronto: Elephant Records, 1990.

Everything you'd want to sing about—from A to Z.
Songs included: "Grandpa's Farm," "Mister Sun."

Sweet Honey in the Rock. *All for Freedom*. Redway, Ca.: Earthbeat Records, 1992.

Songs from Africa and America, both traditional and original, that celebrate the African-American musical tradition and culture.
Songs included: "Down in the Valley."

Warren-Mattox, Cheryl, Varnette P. Honeywood, and Brenda Joysmith. *Shake It to the One You Love: Play Songs and Lullabies from Black Music Traditions*. Booklet included. San Francisco: Warren-Mattox Productions, 1989.

A professional, beautiful tape filled with songs that echo the days of our childhoods.
Songs included: "All the Pretty Little Horses."

Winter, Cathy. *Travelling Home*. Albany: Flying Fish Records, 1988.

Original songs by this New York State artist.
Songs included: "Canoer's Lullaby."

Bluestein, Gene. *The Voice of the Folk; Folklore and American Literary Theory.* Amherst: University of Massachusetts Press, 1972.

A scholarly examination of the sources and theories of folklore, including the sources of American Folk Songs.

Botkin, B. A., ed. *A Treasury of American Folklore: Stories, Ballads and Traditions of the People.* Foreword by Carl Sandburg. New York: Crown Publishers, 1944.

A long, scholarly examination of American folklore in all its aspects, with pages of information, stories, and songs.

_____. *The American Play-Party Song.* New York: Frederick Ungar Publishing Co., 1937.

An eclectic collection of games and songs, many that have come to be deeply ingrained in American playgrounds, schools, and homes.

Fowke, Edith Fulton, comp. and ed. *Ring Around the Moon.* New York: Prentice-Hall, 1977.

A collection, from a variety of primary sources of children's songs, with notes.

_____. *Sally Go Round the Sun.* Music arrangements by Keith MacMillan, illustrated by Carlos Marchiori. Garden City, N.Y.: Doubleday, 1969.

Children's games and songs, collected from primary sources, with notes on the sources and the uses of the songs.

Fox, Dan, arrang. and ed. *Go In and Out the Window: An Illustrated Songbook for Young People.* Commentary by Claude Marks. Illustrated with art works from The Metropolitan Museum's collection. New York: The Metropolitan Museum of Art, Henry Holt & Co., 1987.

A handsome volume, containing classic and familiar songs of America.

Glazer, Tom. *Eye Winker, Tom Tinker, Chin Chopper: Fifty Music Fingerplays.* Illustrated by Ron Himler. Garden City, N.Y.: Doubleday & Co., 1972.

Fifty classic fingerplays, some with Glazer's own twist, all with directions.

Hart, Jane, comp. *Singing Bee! A Collection of Favorite Children's Songs*. Illustrated by Anita Lobel. New York: Lothrop, Lee & Shepard Books, 1982.

Among the more than one hundred songs are lullabies, holiday songs, traditional songs, singing games and fingerplays.

Jenkins, Ella. *The Ella Jenkins Song Book for Children*. Illustrated by Peggy Lischutz. Piano accompaniments by Sherman Krane. New York: Oak Publications, 1966.

Songs sung by a classic children's programmer.

Jones, Bessie, and Bess Lomax Hawes. *Step It Down: Games, Plays, Songs, and Stories from the Afro-American Heritage*. New York: Harper & Row, 1972.

A wide-ranging collection, compiled in an anecdotal yet comprehensive manner, of African-American musical folk heritage. Contains musical notation, words, and directions for many songs and games.

Langstaff, Nancy, and John Langstaff, comps. *Jim Along, Josie: A Collection of Folk Songs and Singing Games for Young Children*. Piano arrangements by Seymour Barab, guitar chords by Happy Traum. Illustrated by Jan Pienkowski. New York: Harcourt Brace Jovanovich, Inc., 1970.

Folk songs, action games, and singing games make up this collection.

Lomax, Alan. *The Land Where the Blues Began*. New York: Pantheon, 1993.

By an eminent folklorist and musicologist, this is an impressive historical survey of black music in America.

_____, ed. *The Folk Songs of North America in the English Language*. Garden City, N.Y.: Doubleday, 1960.

Words, music and origins of over three hundred folk songs, celebrating things like love, work, the sea, and the prairie.

Lomax, John A., and Alan Lomax, comps. *American Ballads and Folk Songs*. With a foreword by George Lyman Kittredge. New York: Macmillan, 1934.

A chapter on songs of childhood contains many classic songs.

_____, collects., adapts., arrangs., *111 Best American Ballads: Folk Song, U.S.A.* Edited by Alan Lomax, music editing by Charles Seeger and Ruth Crawford Seeger. New York: Duell, Sloan and Pearce, 1947.

A foreword, as well as the sections in the front of each chapter of songs, are filled with information about the songs' origins and meanings.

Newell, William Wells, comp. *Games and Songs of American Children*. With introduction and index by Carl Withers. New York: Dover Publications, 1963.

A serious study about the nature and origin of children's play.

Palmer, Hap. *Baby Songs: A Collection of Songs for the Very Young from the Videos "Baby Songs" and "More Baby Songs."* Illustrated by Susannah Ryan. New York: Crown Publishers, 1990.

Songs about everything important to baby, from bathtime to mealtime.

Quackenbush, Robert, comp. and illus. *The Holiday Song Book*. Musical arrangements by Harry Buch. New York: Lothrop, Lee & Shepard, 1977.

A celebration of twenty-seven holidays with one hundred songs.

Raffi. *The Raffi Singable Songbook: A Collection of Fifty-One Songs from Raffi's First Three Records for Young Children*. Illustrations by Joyce Yamamoto. New York: Crown Publishers, 1980.

A collection of songs as well-known as Raffi.

_____. *The Second Raffi Songbook*. Illustrated by Joyce Yamamoto. New York: Crown Publishers, 1986.

More songs from that favorite children's singer.

Reynolds, Malvina. *The Malvina Reynolds Songbook*. Illustrated by Emmy Lou Packard. Berkeley, CA: Schroeder Music Company, 1974.

A collection of songs as diverse and eclectic as they are singable and enjoyable. From protest and environmental songs to lullabies.

Seeger, Pete. *American Favorite Ballads*. New York: Oak Publications, 1961.

Classic ballads from America's troubadour.

Seeger, Ruth Crawford. *American Folk Songs for Children in Home, School and Nursery School: A Book for Children, Parents, and Teachers*. Illustrated by Barbara Cooney. Garden City, N.Y.: Doubleday & Co., 1948.

An introduction to using songs with children, several different indexes, as well as ninety childhood folk songs. A classic collection by a pioneer in the field of children's programming.

_____. *Animal Folk Songs by Children: Traditional American Songs*. Illustrated by Barbara Cooney. Garden City, N.Y.: Doubleday, 1950.

Folk songs about all creatures, great, small, and in-between with an introduction and notes on additional verses for many songs.

Sharon, Lois, and Bram. *The All New Elephant Jam.* Illustrated by David Shaw. New York: Crown Publishers, 1989.

Songs from several of their recordings brought together in a print collection.

_____. *Sharon, Lois, and Bram's Mother Goose: Songs, Finger Games, Tickling Verses, Games, and More.* Illustrated by Mary Ann Kovalski. Boston: Atlantic Monthly Press, 1985.

Just what the title says—songs, finger games, and fun.

Wilder, Alec. *Lullabies and Night Songs.* Illustrated by Maurice Sendak, edited by William Engvick. New York: Harper & Row, 1965.

Lullabies from around the world as well as original songs.

Winn, Marie, collect. and ed. *The Fireside Book of Children's Songs.* Musical arrangements by Allan Miller, illustrated by John Alcorn. New York: Simon & Schuster, 1966.

Over one hundred favorites divided into five sections from lullabies to rounds.

_____, collect. and ed. *The Fireside Book of Fun and Game Songs.* Musical arrangements by Allan Miller, illustrated by Whitney Darrow, Jr. New York: Simon & Schuster, 1974.

Ever kind of song you can think of—from "spur of the moment" songs to "clapping, snapping, and making peculiar noises" songs.

_____, collect. and ed. *What Shall We Do and Allee Galloo! Play Songs and Singing Games for Young Children.* Musical Arrangements by Allan Miller, illustrated by Karla Kuskin. New York: Harper & Row, 1970.

Songs that invite movement, from "follow-the-leader" songs to "simple games."

Yolen, Jane, ed. *The Fireside Song Book of Birds and Beasts.* Arranged by Barbara Green, illustrated by Peter Parnall. New York: Simon & Schuster, 1972.

A celebration of all kinds of wildlife in song.

Song Indexes

Title Index of All Songs

Title Index of Preschooler Songs

Title Index of Family Songs

First Line Index
Preschool Songs

First Line Index
Family Songs

Subject Index to All Songs

Aside from the general headings and categories into which all of the songs have been grouped, this index will help to guide you to songs under a few, more specific subjects. Although there are probably more possible subject headings for these songs than the six listed here, these should prove to be useful without becoming too specific. They are Animals, Counting, Love, Outdoors, Pretend, and Traditional. Some songs are listed more than once. Some are not included in these groups at all.

Love Songs

Outdoors Songs

Pretend Songs